INDO-AMERICAN RELATION DURING UPA-I GOVERNMENT

FEROZE AHMAD MIR

ISBN-10:1541294963

ISBN-13:978-1541294967

DEDICATION

This book is dedicated to my parents, teachers and friends.

CONTENTS

Acknowledgement

All praises to almighty Allah for bestowing me self-confidence and courage, which made this dissertation a successful one.

First and foremost, I would like to acknowledge my indebtedness to my supervisor **Dr. Narendra Ojha**, Department of Pol. Science M.L.B. Girls College Indore, for being exceptionally nice to me throughout my research. This study would have never been accomplished without his painstaking, humble and excellent guidance through all the stages of my research.

I am extremely grateful to **Dr. Kanhiya Ahuja,** H.O.D. School of Social Science and **Dr. Narendra Ojha**, coordinator, Department of Pol. Science, Devi Ahilya University, Indore for their intellectual support and encouragement. I will be failing in my duties if I will not express my thanks to my teachers, **Prof. Narendra Ojha**, **Prof. Sanjay Jain**, **Dr. Ashwani Sharma,** of Pol. Science department for their support and for developing healthy academic environment in the department.

I would like to express my thanks to my well-wishers Dr. **Shabnum Khan and Shakeela Khan** who had been the torch bearer for me throughout the course of this study. I cannot afford ignoring the contribution of them for their encouragement and support. They helped me during the course of field work and compilation of the project. I also wish to thank my friends and beloved roommates **(Ishfaq Farooq Lone, Suhail Ahmad Wani, Mohammad Ashraf Meer, Sheikh Majid and Tawfeeq Ahmad).**

I am also thankful to my colleagues at the Department for their kind assistance at various stages of my research. I am thankful to the research scholars of the Pol. Science department, **Ishfaq Farooq Lone, Tariq Ahmad, Shahee Firdous, Parvaiz Ahmad.** My special thanks to **Ishfaq Farooq Lone, Dr. Suhail Ahmad Wani, Mohd. Ashraf Meer** for assisting me in the typing of the present work for giving their insightful comments and ably assisting me in the completion of various tasks associated with this work.

Moreover, I wish to acknowledge and give thanks to the staff of Devi Ahilya University Library, Delhi University Library, University of Kashmir Library, Jawahar Laal Nehru Library, Jammia Millia Islamia Library, and Teen Morti Library for helping me in getting the necessary material for my research work. I am also thankful to the officials and non-teaching department of school of social science who kept me updated.

I am thankful to my cousin brothers (**Suhail Ahmad, Raashid Hussain, Mohammad Anees, Yasir Habib, Mohammad Younis, Junaid Ahmad and Dawood Ahmad)** and cousin sisters, (**Masroofa, Iqra, Ruqia, Fozia, Kulsuma, and Pakeeza)** who accompanied me during the field-work and assisted me in conducting interviews. I am deeply indebted to them for their whole hearted co-operation in many ways during the field work and for their moral support and co-operation and for making Indore a memorable place for me.

I wish to express my heartfelt appreciation to my uncle **Mr. Khazir Mohammad, Habib-ullah, Mohammad Hussain, Gh. Mohammad and Shahnawaz Ahmad.** who always played the role of guardian throughout my life. I am thankful to them for their critical role in getting access to necessary information and documents which were invaluable inputs in my work.

Finally, with a profound sense of gratitude and love I must express the kind and generous support that I have been receiving from my beloved parents, **Mohammad Ayoob Mir** and my beloved mother, **Rafeeqa Begum**. Their blessings have remained a constant source of enlightenment in all my academic endeavors. I dedicate the present work to them. I am grateful to my brothers, **Ishtiyaq Ahmad Mir** as he is the pillar of strength upon which my life is built. Heartfelt thanks to the whole of my beloved family, which has been a source of joy and solace for me all through the entire career and especially my sister **Mehnaza Akther** for her emotional support throughout the study period.

I am grateful to all the respondents for their co-operation and overwhelming response to the interviews without which the present work would not have been accomplished.

Finally, I am very much indebted to all those who have directly and indirectly been associated towards the completion of the present work.

Feroze Ahmad Mir

Chapter 1ˢᵗ
HISTORICAL BACKGROUND

(Pre Independence Period)

"We shall not realize our objective unless we are willing to help free people to maintain their free institutions and their national integrity against aggressive movements that seek to impose upon them totalitarian regimes. This is no more than a frank recognition that totalitarian regimes imposed on free peoples by direct are indirect aggression, undermine the foundations of international peace and hence the security of U.S. The U.S has made frequent protests against coercion and intimidation in violation of the Yalta agreement in the Poland, Rumania and Bulgaria..... I believe that it must be the policy of the U.S to support free peoples who are attempted subjugation by armed minorities or by outside pressures. We must take immediate and resolute action. The free peoples of the world look to us for support in maintaining their freedom. If we falter in our leadership, we may in danger the peace of the world, and we shall surely endanger the welfare of our own nation." (President Truman, Truman Doctrine- March 1947)

Before the Indian independence India had no diplomatic relations with USA, because India's foreign policy was being guided by the British government in those days. Beside the America had adopted a policy of isolation before the First World War (1914-1918). She had no interest in any other country of Asia except China and Japan. Though America had no interest in India before the first Great War, yet two great religious leaders of India Swami Vivekananda and Swami

Ram Tirtha had visited America and removed many misunderstandings about Hindu religion and culture in the minds of American people by their fiery and eloquent speeches. In 1911 Lala Hardiyal had founded a Gadar party in America and prepared thousands of Indians for liberation struggle of their country. When the world war began in 1914, Gadar party sent hundred men to India, so that they might stir up a revolt here. But they did not succeed.[1]

Mark Twain visited India in 1896 and described it in his travelogue following the equator with both revulsion and attraction before concluding that India was the only land he dreamed about or longed to see again.[2]

The historical links between the United States and India can be traced to the year 1492- i.e. to the year when Christopher Columbus discovered the America in the course of his search for a new route to India. Formal relation however, did not begin until India achieved its Independence on 15 August 1947. It is from this time that the official relations between India and the United States can be traced. Prior to this, "American contacts with India had started before the American Revolution through soldiers and seamen who had lived both in the American Colonies and in India.[3] Till the first half of the 19th century several American ships, trading within the limits as permitted by the East Indian Company's monopoly, visited Indian ports. But Americans had little curiosity to know about the intellectual life, history and politics of India. Neither America nor India learned anything about each other.[4]

---

[1] Verma. H.M and Kulshrestha, M.M. Approach to Indian Foreign Policy and World Affairs. Gwalior: Nidhi Prakashan, 1997-98. P-172.

[2] htpp// en.m.wikipedia.org/wiki:/india-united states-relations. Acess on 23-02 2014.

[3] Tewari,S.C.Indo-US- Relations1947-1976 . New Delhi: Radiant Publishers, 1977. P- 1.

[4] Chaturshreni, Ved Vati. Indo-US Relations. New Delhi: National Publishing

The two regions, so distant from each other, were parts of the expanding British Empire and were already the brightest jewels in the British crown. Shortly after American Revolution, the first American merchantman landed at Indian ports, first at Pondicherry and Calcutta and soon enterprising American businessmen had established contacts and entered into agreements with the British and French firms in India (their contacts with Indians were few and unimportant). In the famous Jays' Treaty of 1794, the United States obtained special concessions for trade in India from the British government. American trade with India, a part of the "China Trade," continued to be important through the early years of the 19th Century and the clipper ship era. Thereafter that it languished and was succeed by other types of business relationships in the late 19th Century and into the 20th Century.[5] With the establishment of the American board of commissionaires for foreign mission in 1810, the first American missionaries-Mr. and Mrs. Judson, Mr. and Mrs. Newell, Mr. and Mrs. Nott, Mr. Gorden Hall, and Mr. Rice sailed for India in the 1812. They were not permitted by East Indian Company to land in settle down in India. But to their good luck in 1813, the East Indian India Company was granted a new charter. This charter said that Christian Missionaries should be allowed to carry on their work in India. This enabled the American Missionaries to being their activities on a permanent basis.[6] In 1815, the American Mahratta Mission was established. Missionary activities in India and their observations about the people of Indian subcontinent gave firsthand information about India to the Americans. The main interest of the missionaries was to establish schools and distribute religious literature in the various Indian languages. They preached the Christian faith at street corners. They gradually enlarged their activities and their number went on increasing. The number of missionaries in India in 1885 was 139.[7]

House. 1973. P- 36.

[5] Sinha, Ajoy. Indo-US Relations. New Delhi: Janki Prakashan, 1994. PP- 3,4.

[6] Tewari, S. n-3. P 2.

Some American Missionaries did a lot of humanitarian work during the Indian famines of 1897 and 1899. They were helpful in persuading American public opinion of the need to assist India in coping with its acute food shortage. The American people made generous contribution to the cause of fighting the famines.[8] As late as 1892, there were only 394American Missionaries in India. The number rose to 1,025 by 1903 and to a peak of 2478 in 1922. Thereafter, as the Indian national movement gathered momentum, their numbers, activities and influence declined, with some significant personal exceptions. They have not fared well in independent India. But the memory of their work lingers on in both India and the United States, and while in both countries the images and impressions of that work are mixed and episodic, American Missionaries helped to form the "scratches on our minds" noted by Harold Issues when he made his study of American images of India.[9]

Lala Lajpat Rai was the first India's political leader who visited United States in 1905. He went there in order to tell the American people about the need for Indian Independence. In 1916 a book written by him in the United States and entitled. The United States of America: A Hindu's impression was published by R. Chaterjee, Editor of the Modern Review. This book was the first of its kind to be written by an Indian in the United States. Lala Lajpat Rai was much influenced by American life and American Democratic Institutions. He felt that the Indian student could learn a lot from the United States.[10] Lajpat Rai spent almost five years in America, lecturing widely and attracting many American leaders to sympathize with two Indian national position, including J .T Sunderland, a Unitarian minister who had visit India 1895-96 and later 1913-14. In 1919,

---

[7] Natrajan, L. American Christian Mission in India in the 19th Century .Calcutta: Modern review, 1964. P-43.

[8] Ibid, PP- 2, 3.

[9] Sinha, Ajoy. Indo-Us Relations. New Delhi: Janki Prakashan, 1994. PP- 4, 5.

[10] Tewari, S.C. n-3, PP- 4, 5.

Sunderland wrote India in Bondage, which received an enthusiastic welcome in India.[11] One of the first to arrive in the US was Taraknath Das, who came in 1906 to study at the University of Washington following his release from the so called 1917 Hindu conspiracy case conviction; he organized the friends of freedom for India, which attracted the support of many Americans.[12]

Lajpat Rai was a great admirer of the USA. He was however, provoked to write something against in his book "Un happy India" written in reply to Katherine Mayo's book 'Mother India' (published in 1927). Katherine Mayo was an American lady who visited India during the winter of 1925-26. She had given a much distorted picture of India in her book Mother India. She had given a dark account of Indian life and culture. The book thus created a wrong and bad impression about India among the American people. A majority of Americans thought of India as a land of Sannyasis, naked ascetics, be jeweled princes and poor people. The book got wide publicity in America. It went through as many as thirteen editions from May 1927 to January1928. It created tremendous misunderstanding between India and United States.[13]

Support to Indian nationalism came from varied quarters. William Jenings Brayan had visited India in 1906 and returning home, criticized British rule on the grounds that it served only British interests. In 1925, the Rev John Hayne Holmes journeyed to India where in western clothes but wearing a "Gandhi Cap" he addressed the annual meeting of the Indian National Congress.[14] One of the most active and influential of the religious leaders to espouse the Indian cause was the Reverend John Haynes Holmes, pastor of the community church in New York. In

---

[11] Patil ,V.T and Assiananda, Sri. A Case Study of US South Asian Relation 1942-1965. New Delhi: Minerva Press, 2002. PP-161,162.

[12] Ibid, P- 161.

[13] Tewari, S.C. n-3, PP-5, 6.

[14] Patil, V.T. n-11, P- 162.

1921 he preached a famous sermon on Gandhi, whom he called "the greatest man in the world today." From his pulpit and on May public rostrums, he praised Gandhi and other Indian leaders.[15]

The role played by US in helping India's struggle for freedom is not generally known in this country. Yet it is true that since the early part of this century, the Indian Independence movement received the active moral and material support of the American People. The United States was a sanctuary for some prominent freedom fighters of India. These include eminent scholars, Journalists, Scientists and thinkers. Important among them were Silendra Naath Ghosh, Dhangopal Muookerjee, Syed Hussain, Haridas Majumdar, M.N Roy, B.K Sarkar, R.C Bajpai, Judge Saund and Krishanlal Shridnarani. Indian nationalists derived much inspiration in their fight against British Rule from American leaders and citizens.[16]

After 1920, a change started taking place in the thinking of Americans because of the increasing influence of Mahatma Gandhi on the Indian political scene. It was because of his political philosophy of non-violence and non-cooperation that a good number of Americans began to look sympathetically towards the Indian National movement for Independence.[17] Gandhi's civil disobedience movement in the 1930's attracted much attention in America and his defiance of the salt tax was compared in the America press to the Boston tea party. More than 20 books were published on India in 1930 indicating the interest in the country of these, William James Durant's the case for India and Gertude Emerson's voiceless India was the most persuasive.[18]

---

[15] Sinha, Ajoy. n-5, P- 9.

[16] Tewari ,S.c. n-3 PP- 7,8.

[17] Chaturshreni, Ved Vati. n-4, P- 37.

[18] V, Patil. n-14, P- 162.

For all the ignorance of and indifference to the nationalist struggle in India on the part of the most American's at least one image came through strongly if not always clearly. That was the image of Mahatma Gandhi. It was a confused image, ranging all the way from administration for the little man in the lion cloth who defined the might of the Britain the Indian David facing the mighty British Goriath-railed the Indian people in the support of the Independence struggle and taught them the methods of civil disobedience, to distrust of the "naked fakir," to use Churchill's words, who spoke in parables about 'Truth' and ahimsa and satyagraha and created problems for Britain and its vast Empire at the time when, in American eyes, far greater threats then those posed by a dying colonialism were appearing on the international scene. But on the whole Gandhiji's image was a favorable one among those Americans who were at all concerned with the world events.[19]

The Indians regarded USA as the home of democracy, and hoped that it would help in their aspiration for liberty. After the world war first Woodrow Wilson, the President of America, proposed the right of self-determination at the Paris Peace Conference. The Indian leaders welcomed the move with great applause as they hoped that this principle shall be adopted in the case of India also. Pandit Madan Mohan Malviya, the President of the Delhi Congress session in 1919, called Wilson as the messenger of God for the establishment of peace.[20]

During the First World War the supporters of the Indian struggle for freedom were subjected to ill treatment by the US government. Few American Organizations had courage enough to the support the Indian cause. In spite of this contribution of the American people towards India's struggle for freedom, the attitude of the U.S government was very discouraging .The U.S government did

---

[19] Sinha ,Ajoy. n-5, PP- 8,9.

[20] Verma, H.M and Kulshrestha, M.M. n-1, PP- 172,173.

not want to displease the British government. However, the American people viewed the matter from an entirely different angle.[21]

---

[21] Tewari, S.C. n-3, P- 9.

Chapter 2nd

INDO AMERICAN RELATIONS DURING COLD WAR ERA (1945-1990)

As the United States and the former Soviet Union unleashed a cold war that effected to varying degrees the entire gamut of international relations, the different national and foreign policy priorities of India and the United States under the given circumstances prevented the two from having the best of relations with each other.[22]

When India became independent, many leaders regarded USA as an Imperialist country and viewed it with suspicion. Those were the days, when a cold war was going on between America and Russia. America had adopted an attitude that the countries, which were not openly on the side of America, were against her.[23]

In late 1947, shortly after India and Pakistan became independent, the dispute over Kashmir flared up into warfare between the new nations in the subcontinent and became internationalized when, in early 1948, India brought the question before the U.N Security Council. India was quite unhappy with the position taken by the United States on this question, which is regarded as anti-India and pro Pakistan.[24]

In the year 1946, India faced an acute food shortage. American leaders evinced much interest in solving the Indian food crisis. The Presidents famine Emergency Committee appointed Hebert Hoover, a former President of the USA,

---

[22] Chintamani, Mahapatra. Indo-US Relations into the 21st Century. New Delhi: Knowledge World, 1998. P- 36.

[23] Verma. H.M and Kulshrestha.M.M. Approach to Indian Foreign Policy and World Affairs. Nidhi Prakashan: Gwalior, 1997-1998. P- 173.

[24] Sinha, Ajoy. Indo US Relations. New Delhi: Janki Prakashan, 1994. P- 13.

to tour in May 1946 and makes a survey of the Indian food situation. On 16th May 1946 the USA and India concluded an agreement under the agreement the USA sent many food shipments to India. The next formal agreement to be concluded was the United States Air Transport Agreement of 14 November 1946. This established a direct link between two countries.[25]

India and America came closer to each other by Shri Jawaharlal Nehru's visit to America in October, 1949. Thereafter some misunderstandings arose but they were removed gradually. From January, 1951 a new era of co-operation between the two countries began, when US educational foundation was established in India. In February 1951 India was faced with an acute shortage of food grains. On the request of India, President Truman appealed to the American Senate to give a free help to India of 20 lac tons of food grain. On 15th June, 1951 Truman signed the Indian Emergency Food Assistance Act by which America gave help to India for the first time. From June, 1951 to April 1971 America gave to India financial Assistance of 7422 corers 23 lacs of Rupees. This help was given in the form of loans and grants. It includes a grant of 115 Corers 28 Lacs of Rupees, which was not to be repaid by Indian government.[26]

India became independent at a time when the tendency towards polarization had already set in the world politics. The cold war between the two United States and the Soviet Union constituted to a very extent the external policy environment of countries like India. India revolted against the implications of the cold war which drastically restricted its freedom of action. Being engrossed in its own complex domestic problems, it did not play an important role in international politics. Even in those in vital years it sought to develop friendly bilateral relations with the United States.[27]

---

[25] Tewari, S C. Indo US Relations 1947-1976. New Delhi: Random Publishers, 1977. PP- 17, 18.

[26] Verma. H.M and Kulshrestha, M.M.. n-2, PP- 177,178.

US India relations have vacillated between 'cold' and 'warm' since India became a free nation in 1947. Interestingly, they have never reached a point of either downright hostility or an unflinching love affair, unlike the US relation with chin for instance.[28]

India did not try the line dictated by USA in the period of cold war, but adopted independent foreign Policy based on the principles of Non-Alignment.[29] Non-Alignment means non-involvement with any military group or bloc. India is Non-Aligned and uncommitted to certain policies and objectives which may give it an appearance of neutrality. Nehru reiterated this policy on 8 March 1949, and said India would be friends with all neighboring countries and would not join any alliances. Non-Alignment does not mean "neutrality" is wrong except during the war. India is not therefore, a country following a policy of neutrality.[30]

The United States has entered into military alliances with a number of countries and has established military bases in those countries. India is fundamentally opposed to such a policy. It is the pursuit of such a policy by the United States which has been responsible for the many ups and downs in Indo-US relations. Since India became independent. In 1949, the NATO was formed at the instance of the United States. In 1951, the U.S joined mutual defense pacts with Australia, Newzealand and the Philippines. It also entered into pacts with Japan, South Korea and Nationalist China. In 1954, it entered into a military agreement

---

[27] Prasad, Bimal. India's Foreign Policy. New Delhi: Vikas Publishing House, 1979. P- 1.

[28] Kapur, Ashok, Malik ,Y.K, Gould, Harld A and Rubinoff, Arthur G. India and United States In a Changing World. New Delhi: Sage Publication, 2002. P- 1.

[29] Zia, Rakib Ahmad. International Relations: Theory and Practice. Srinagar: Ali Mohammad and Sons, 2006. P-316.

[30] Brown, W.Norman. The United States Of India and Pakistan. Cambridge: Mass publication, 1963. P- 364.

with Pakistan. In view of the success of the communists in taking over North Vietnam, the United States organized the SEATO in September 1954. It encouraged the formation of the Baghdad pact in 1955 without joining it. India considered all these moves as fundamentally wrong. Because of this, the United States has been apathetic, if not positively hostile, to Indian interests in matters like Kashmir and Goa.[31]

India's formal independence in August 1947 did engender hopes for amicable and constructive ties. These hopes however were soon tampered with the Indo-Pakistan war over Kashmir in 1948 caused the first significant disillusionment. On the advice of the British and American government, India went on good faith to the United Nations with a complaint of aggression against Pakistan. But the Anglo American 'experts' converted it into an Indo-Pak 'dispute' and enlarged its scope. Instead of asking Pakistan to vacate the areas forcibly and illegally occupied by it in the State of Jammu and Kashmir, which had duly acceded to India, they succeeded in imposing a cease fire and appointing a UN Kashmir Commission. This was a device to bring both Pakistan and India under Anglo-American influence and if India proved 'obdurate' then to weaken her by supporting Pakistan.[32]

In June, 1950 North Korea attacked South Korea USA came forward with a resolution condemning North Korea as an aggressor and asking UNO to send its forces there. India supported the resolution and it was carried by a majority. America had hoped that India would send her troops to Korea, but India did not send her soldiers, because she did not want aggravate trouble. Subsequently China sent her army to help North Korea. Under the changed circumstances USA brought a resolution at the Security Council condemning

---

[31] Tewari, S C. n-4, PP- 28, 29.

[32] Kaul, T.N. Reminiscence Discree and in Discreat. New Delhi: Lancer Publisher, 1982. PP- 270, 271.

China as an aggressor. India opposed it strongly; hence the relation between India and USA were strained and India's policy was criticized severely in America.[33]

On 20 July, 1951 the government of USA sent a draft to 51 Countries, who had fought against Japan during the Second World War, and invited these Countries to a conference at San Francisco. The government of India considered the draft to be strict and suggested some amendments, which were not acceptable to President Truman. India refused a separate Treaty with Japan on 9th June, 1952 and thus there was great resentment America.[34] In 1954-1955 India and the United States became further estranged over Indo-China. India was critical of French activities in the part of South East Asia and of US support of the French. It also blamed the United States for the India's exclusion from participation in the Geneva Conference in 1955 that tried to reach an agreement on the future of Vietnam after the French defeat.[35] India was in favor of a peaceful solution. When there was open warfare in Indo-China, Nehru put forth a six-point proposal. USA interpreted it quite wrongly and thought that Nehru was trying to save the Communist leader, Ho Chi Minch from inevitable defeat. When there was a conference at Geneva for putting an end to the war, Dulles tried to make the conference failure. But with the help of India to conference was successful. There was a serious reaction to it in America.[36] After the traumatic experience of the Korean War, the United States decided on a more aggressive policy for the maintenance of its global hegemony an, failing to get Indian support for it, entered into a military alliance with Pakistan in 1954. Consequently, it had to share to some extent the regional foreign- policy objectives of its ally Pakistan, which had cast itself in the role of an adversely of India. The policy of support for Pakistan and opposition to China pulled US policy in South Asia in two opposite

[33] Verma. H.M and Kulshrestha, M.M. n-2, P-175.

[34] Ibid, P- 175.

[35] Sinha, Ajoy. n-3, P- 18.

[36] Verma. H.M and Kulshrestha, M.M. n-2, P-175.

directions. Us alliance with Pakistan forced India to seek Soviet support to reinforce its own position. As India's need for Soviet support grew as a result of US policies, Soviet influence in India increased. India however, never became totally dependent on the Soviet Union, nor did it ever give up its search for good relation with the United States.[37]

During the two major World crisis of 1956, India and the United States were both opposed to the Anglo-French-Israeli invasion of Egypt, but they were far apart in their reactions to the Hungarian cries, with the United States immediately and strongly denouncing the soviet invasion and brutalities in Hungary, and with India delaying for several weeks before Nehru came out with relatively mild expression of disapproval of the soviet action.[38]

The events of the previous two year provided a rather unpropitious backdrop for Nehru's second official visit to United States in December 1956. This visit, however, went off unexpectedly; well at least in its public aspect. Nehru was in a better mood than in 1949, and he and President Eisenhower apparently established a good working relationship. in public statement, Nehru called Eisenhower a man of peace, and he referred to the "friendly and cordial relation" that had existed between India and America "even before India gained her independence" Eisenhower was a gracious host, who praised Nehru and India for adhering to the democratic path in their efforts at nation building. In his memoirs observed that too many Americans Nehru seemed to be "a somewhat inexplicable and occasionally exasperating personality.[39] Undoubtedly, the meeting of Nehru and Eisenhower generated a lot of goodwill on both sides and it marked a watershed in the relations between U.S.A. and India. The president was struck by Nehru's great sincerity in his passion for peace. He could see why it was necessary

---

[37] Prasad, Bimal. n-6, P- 382.

[38] Sinha ,Ajoy. n-3, P 19.

[39] Ibid.P-19.

for countries like India to have a period of at least ten to fifteen years continuous peace in and around them to work for removal of poverty from their midst. Eisenhower during his meeting on the second day told Nehru how he had, after their talks on the previous day, already started parading his knowledge of South Asian situation and about Nehru's argument of nationalism emerging stronger then communism in Yugoslavia and Poland from then onwards, there was a perceptible appreciation of India's key position in Asia. The US administration began seriously to consider how India should be further helped and her key position fostered to save Asia and eventually Europe and the United States.[40]

Three years later, President Eisenhower made a state visit to India, which turned out to be for more than a routine affair. He received a tumultuous welcome. At this reception Nehru hailed Eisenhower as "a great man and the representative of a great country and nation," and he told his famous guest that, "India has given you her most valuable thing-a part of her heart." Eisenhower responded warmly, he declared that India and the United States "ought to be closer." His Indian visit made a deep impression on him. His visit undoubtedly helped to improve the tone of Indo American relations, but its influence improving the basic relation between the two countries should not be exaggerated.[41]

Better Indo US Relations were expected during John F. Kennedy's presidentship. His approach to the Third World Countries was more humanitarian than political. He believed that economic stability in these countries would lead to political stability and check the spread of Communism. Thus he thought India could be wooed by the US through the substantial economic aid. During Kennedy's tenure India received more than 50% of aid from U.S.A but when the question of assistance for the Bokaro steel plant arose the clay commission

---

[40] Rana, A.P. Four Decades of Indo US Relations. New Delhi: Har Anand Publications, 1994. P-12.

[41] Sinha, Ajoy. n-3, PP- 19, 20.

suggested that the United States should not aid a foreign government in projects establishing government owned industrial and commercial enterprises which compete with existing private sector Endeavour[42].

When India got freedom on 15th of August, 1947 the British supremacy was gone, but there were some French and Portuguese possessions in India. Subsequently French entrusted Pondicherry, Yanam, Mahe and Karikal to government of India. But Portugal was not willing to give back Goa, Daman, Diu and Nagar Haveli. Since popular opinion was against the retention of these colonies, India could not allow the question of Goa to linger on. Hence on 18th December, 1961 India took recourse to military action. Within two days the Portuguese colonies got emancipation from the foreign yoke. When there was a discussion at UNO on India's action the U.S. representative, Adlai Stevenson expressed the anger of America in the following words, "Tonight we are witnessing the first act of a drama that could end with its (United Nations) death." He criticized Ceylon, Egypt and others, who supported the Indian move .India, did not like the America's support to colonialism.[43]

During 1960's that the two Countries India and USA moved towards reapproachment, because of growing tensions in India's relation with China. Since Communist China posed a potent threat to the US supremacy, the China Indian border war of 1962 provided a golden opportunity to the United States to co-operate, with India on security matters. Accordingly, a high level co-operation, between India and United States marked this period.[44] Congress party members warmly expressed their thankfulness and gratitude.[45]

---

[42] Malhotra, V.K. Indo-US Relations in Nineties. New Delhi: Anmol Publications, 1995. PP- 8, 9.

[43] Verma. H.M and Kulshrestha, M.M. n-2, PP- 176,177.

[44] Nehru, Jawaharlal. India's Foreign Policy Selected Speeches. September 1946- April 1961, Government of India: P- 305.

Many Indian told Americans that now they knew who their real friends were and viewed that they would never forget the prompt assistance that the United States had provided. This strong pro-American soon began to evaporate, as Indian gradually recovered from the shock of the unexpected Chinese aggression and as a sharp reaction set in because of the joint pressure of the United States and Britain on India and Pakistan to hold a series of meetings to seek a resolution of the Kashmir dispute. Under combined Anglo-American pressure, India and Pakistan had several meetings on Kashmir, but neither country, especially India, was in any mood to compromise and then in late of 1963, the talks were suspended indefinitely.[46]

In 1965 again a twist came into the Indo American relation when Pakistan attacked India with the USA armaments. America remained salient during this, though US did not side either with India or with Pakistan.[47] Some observers were of the opinion that the responsibility for the twin Pakistani aggression of 1965 rested. Wholly with the USA referring to President Eisenhower's assurance in March 1954 that the USA would take action if any one misused American arms, Prime Minister Nehru, expressing his apprehensions, had started: I have no doubt the President is opposed to aggression. But we know from past experience that aggression takes place and nothing is done about it. Aggression may well follow in spite of the best intention of the President and then a long argument will ensure on what exactly is aggression. The US Government after having pumped in an enormous amount of arms into Pakistan found itself unable to prevent Pakistan using them against India.[48]

---

[45] Rana, A.P. n-19, P-41.

[46] Sinha, Ajoy. n-3, P-22.

[47] Chaturshreni, Ved Vati. Indo-US Relations. New Delhi: National Publication, 1987. P- 48.

[48] Rana. A.P. n - 19, PP- 101, 102.

The war left the Indians disillusioned with United States and the Indian Ambassador in Washington B.K Nehru, lodged a strong protest with American Secretary of the State Dean Rusk on September 3, 1965, against the use of US equipment including Patton Tanks, f-86 Sabre jets and F-104 supersonic fighters by Pakistan in Kashmir in violation of the assurance given to the Indian Government by President ship Eisenhower in 1954(that equipment supplied to Pakistan would not be used against India).[49]

In January 1966, Mrs. Indira Gandhi was elected as Shastri's successor as Prime Minister of India. In March 1966, Mrs. Gandhi made an 11 day state visit to the United States, at the invitation of President Johnson, and this visit was pronounced as success in both Countries. At a white House dinner in honor of Mrs. Gandhi, Johnson proposed that an Indo-US Educational Foundation be established, to be financed mainly from counterpart funds credited to the US Government from the rupees that had accumulated from the sale of PL-480 shipments of food grains.[50] Another dispute between the India and America erupted when India refused to sign the nuclear Non-proliferation Treaty (NPT) OF 1968.[51]

After 25th March, 1971 there began a liberation struggle in East Bengal the government of India invited the attention of US government that American arms were being used by Pakistan in killing thousands of Bengalis. Due to this there was a heavy flow of refugees from East Bengal to India which had caused a heavy burden to the Indian finances. India asked the USA to put pressure on the President of Pakistan Yahya Khan so that the genocide in East Bengal could be stopped. But the President Nixon said that it is the internal affair of Pakistan so

---

[49] Ibid, P- 102.

[50] Sinha, Ajoy. n-3, PP- 25, 26.

[51] Limaye, Satu P. US Indian Relations: The Pursuit of Accommodation . Boulder: West View Press, 1993. P- 19.

that he could not interfere. Thus it was clear to India that USA is supporting Pakistan in it. On 7th August 1971 India made a strong protest, that in violation of all assurances U.S.A had been supplying arms to Pakistan and had been prompting Pakistan and China to fight against India. At the same time USA had been trying to send its citizens as UN observers in East Bengal. India regarded such activities quite unfriendly.[52] The worst blow to India – US science technology relations during Mrs. Gandhi's regime occurred when India conducted peaceful nuclear explosion on 18 May 1974. Notwithstanding India's claim that its atomic energy would be used for peaceful purpose, the officials in the US administration and Congress demanded to support aiding India and sanctions be imposed.[53]

In the late 1970's with the anti-Soviet Janata Party leader Moraji Desai becoming the Prime Minister, India improved its relations with the US, now led by Jimmy Carter, despite the later signing and order in 1978 baring Nuclear material from being exported to India due to the latter's Non-proliferation record. But again the relation between the two democracies became strained when Mrs. Indira Gandhi returned into power in 1980. The reason for the strained relation was India's support for Soviet invasion and occupation of Afghanistan.[54]

Mrs. Gandhi and her Congress party returned to power in the election of 1980. At about same time, Republican Ronald Regan replaced democrat Jimmy Carter at the White House. Both leaders have different ideologies regarding international relations. But everything changed after the official visit of Mrs. Gandhi to USA in 1982. The two leaders felt comfortable enough with each other to launch one of the most ambitious US-India collaborative research programs called the India United States Science and Technology Initiative (STI) Indian and

---

[52] Verma, H.M and KuulshresthaM.M. n-2 PP- 182, 183.

[53] Kapur,   Ashok, Malik, Y.K.Gould, Harold, A. n-7, P- 48.

[54] htpp//en.m.wikipedia.org/wiki/india-unitedstates-relations. Accessed on 17-03-2014.

American Scientists and research institutions have had many collaborative research projects as separate entities, dating back to the 1950's and 1960's. This new collaboration provided an intergovernmental umbrella that not only helped integrate many of these ongoing programs but also spawned a whole range of new projects where each country was to be an equal participant investment partners.[55]

After the assassination of Mrs. Indira Gandhi in 1984, her son Rajiv Gandhi was elected as the Prime Minister of India. Rajiv Gandhi visited USA in 1985 for five days.[56] Rajiv Gandhi and Ronald Regan met in Washington on June1985 where they extended the agreement of India-United States Science and Technology Initiative (STI) until October 1988. This initiative was the best examples of Science and Technology collaboration between the two nations that may not have always see eye to eye on political matters. The memorandum of understanding on technological co-operation had envisaged that the US would supply the high technology super computer XMP-24 to the Indian Institute of Science, Bangalore to enhance India's weather research capacity program.[57]

In order to strength the Indo-US Relation P.M Rajiv Gandhi paid a short visit to Washington in October 1987. The two Washington gave assurance that it would take necessary steps for preventing Pakistan from becoming Nuclear power State. Despite assurance of US to check Pakistan being a Nuclear State. The US gave 4.2 Billion dollar Military and Economic aid package to Pakistan after the visit of P.M Rajiv Gandhi. It was sharply reacted in India. Expected friendly and co-operative relations between India and America lost its warmth and vigor.[58]

---

[55] Kapur, Ashok. n-17, PP- 51, 52.

[56] Verma. H.M and Kulshrestha, M.M. n-2, P-189.

[57] Kapur, Ashok. n-17, PP- 52, 53.

[58] Verma. H.M and Kulshrestha, M.M. n-2, P- 191.

CHAPTER 3RD

INDO-AMERICAN RELATIONS IN POST COLD WAR ERA (1990-2000)

Relations between India and United States have improved considerably after the end of the cold war. Disintegration of Soviet Union and the US victory in the gulf war, America has emerged as the pre-eminent power in the world. Today's world is dominated and supervised by the US. Some call it as unipolar World. After this change in the World especially after the disintegration of the Soviet Union, there is no super power having sympathy with India, so India has changed its foreign policy after the post-cold war era.[59] As the cold war came to

[59] Malhotra, V.K. Indo-US Relations in Nineties. New Delhi: Anmol Publication, 1995.P-1.

an end, the Soviet troops withdrew from Afghanistan, the Soviet control over East European Countries faded, the Soviet Union underwent a period of internal political chaos and the gulf war took place to liberate Kuwait from Iraqi Military occupation. India during this allowed the American military transport planes to refuel at Bombay's Sahar Airport on their way to the Gulf. This initiative marked the inauguration of much closer level of defense and security understanding between the two countries in subsequent years. There was appreciation in the U.S Policy making circles of India's co-operative action and attitude during the Gulf War.[60]

Two months after the outbreak of the Gulf Crisis, the Bush Administration distanced itself from Pakistan by expressing its inability to certify that country's Nuclear virginity which led the imposition of the presser Amendment and cut-off of all American assistance to Islamabad and in December, 1990, a sizeable American defense delegation, led by Assistant Secretary of Defense for international Security Affairs Henry Rowen, came to India, giving rise to concerns in Islamabad about an American till towards India.[61] Few months after the end of Gulf war, a former commander of the USA Army in the pacific, Claude kicklighter, brought forth a proposal to augment the level of Indo-US defense co-operation in April 1991. This proposal envisaged enhanced level of military-to-military co-operation through joint seminars training and establishment of steering committees. This co-operation was quite different from the kind of defense, ties India had with the former Soviet Union. The prospects of military co-operation received a further boost with the visits of commander-in-chief of the US Pacific command and of the commanding general of the US Army

---

[60] Chintamani, Mahapatra. Indo US-Relations Into 21st Century. New Delhi: Knowledge World, 1998.P-103.

[61] Dixit, J.N. My South Block Years: Memories of Foreign Secretary. New Delhi, Mumbai etc: UBS Publishers, 1996.P-173.

in the Pacific and chief of Naval Operation in October 1991 and January 1992 respectively.[62]

Ever since the military dialogue began, the US has been has keen to have joint military exercises, particularly in the mountainous terrain. Beginning 1991, the two countries have been having joint military exercise, including joint naval exercises which were held in May 1992. India-US service-to-service co-operation saw joint naval drills being conducted in the early year of 1995. Washington even fielded two nuclear powered submarines in these exercise. The US has also expressed its desire to practice with aircraft carriers. The coolest the US came to this was when the US Ambassador, Frank Wisner, in an interview to span magazine in August 1995 stated that the US recognizes the right of the India to have a strong national defense.[63] After the India's refusal to sign various arms control agreements improved relations of 1992 between India and US stalled. In May, India and Russia agreed to collaborate on the Indian Agni missile program to develop rocket and ballistic technologies. This agreement jolted American confidence in India's devotion to arms control. American's response to this agreement was that she threatened to suspend technology and military transfer program to both India and Russia entirely, and temporarily imposed a two year ban on 'sensitive' technology exports to both.[64]

Moreover, with the disintegration of the U.S.S.R, the US began to pressure Russia that she should stall the missile technology to India. Consequently, the President Bori's Yeltsin had to reverse his commitment to the sale, which he had expressed during his New Delhi visit in January 1993, and meekly cancel a

---

[62] Chintamani, Mahapatra. n-2, PP-104, 105.

[63] http://www.idsa-india.org/an-jun-6.html. Accessed on 22-03-2014.

[64] Louscher, David J, Cook, Alethia, H. Military Relations Between the US and India: Assessment Prospects. Ed. Kapur, Ashok, Malik ,Y.K. India and United States in Changing World. New Delhi: Sage Publication, 2002.PP- 311, 312.

large part of the cryogenic rocket technology deal with India. Prior to this US had imposed sanctions on the Indian Space Research Organization (ISRO) and the Russia Space Agency Glaskosmos for two years to slow down India's space program. Indian policy makers, therefore, feel that they cannot accept any agreement that may result in denying India access to modern technology.[65] India's reluctance and the US insistence on signing the Nuclear Non-proliferation Treaty (NPT) or some other regional nuclear non- proliferation arrangement is not a new problem but has been there from the beginning of the NPT. When China, France and South Africa decided to sign the Treaty it has acquired new significance. In past after India's nuclear explosion in 1974, the US has pressurized India on more occasions and in a number of ways to sign NPT.[66] India was not against nuclear non-proliferation, but against one sided obligation and one sided rights and privileges.[67]

India's marginalization on the global scene and its growing nuclear isolation raised some fundamental challenged to Indian nuclear policy by the mid-1990. The debate in Geneva on the drafting of the comprehensive Test Ban Treaty suggested that India's future nuclear weapon options were now being closed. Meanwhile, there was no respite from the United States on high technology related sanctions.[68] The United States encouraged India to sign the

---

[65] Jha, Nalini Kant. "Reviving US-India Friendship in a Changing International Order". Asian Survey, Vol. 34, No. 12, Dec,(1994): 1040.

[66] Malhotra ,V.K. US Latest Initiatives on Non-Proliferation in South Asia and Indo US-Relations, Ed.Dr. Vinay Kumar. Indo-US Relations in Nineties, New Delhi: Anmol Publication, 1995. P- 19.

[67] Dutt ,V.P. India's Foreign Policy in a Changing World. New Delhi: Vikas Publication, 1999. P- 38.

[68] Mohan, C. Raja. The Evolution of India's nuclear Doctrine. Sinha, Atish, Mohta, Madhup. Indian Foreign Policy Challenges and Opportunities. New Delhi: Academic Foundation, 2007. P-1023.

comprehensive Test Ban Treaty (CTBT) immediately and without condition. However, India has yet to sign the CTBT or the NPT, opposing the discriminatory nature of the treaty that allows the five declared nuclear countries of the world to keep their nuclear arsenal and develop it using computer simulation testing. Before to its nuclear testing, India had pressed for a comprehensive destruction of nuclear weapons by all countries of the world in a time-bound frame. India had been adopting independent thinking and has so far not signed NPT and CTBT much against the wishes of USA.[69]

3.1 TRADE AND ECONOMIC RELATIONS

It was only after the institution of an economic liberalization program in June 1991 and disintegration of the Soviet Union in December 1991 that there arose prospects for enhanced level of economic interactions between India and the US. Even before Bill Clinton entered the oval office as the first post-cold war US President in January 1993, a report on India and America after the Cold war, co-authored by senior Carnegie Endowment Associates Selig Harrison and G. Kemp and signed by 34 members of the study group was released, urging the US government to give increased priority to India as the world's largest democracy and as a potential partner in efforts to resolve the global dispute. Another recommendation by the Asia Society Study Mission after the end of cold war to the US government's economic relation should be the focal point of US engagement in South Asia, especially in India.[70]

Such recommendations, infract came in the wake of remarkable transformation in India's economic policies and outlook. When Bill Clinton won

---

[69] Zia, Rakib Ahmad. International Relations; Theory and Practice. Srinagar: Ali Mohammad and Sons, 2006. PP- 316, 317.

[70] Chintamani ,Mahapatra. n-2, PP- 14, 15.

the 1992 US Presidential election, a mini economic revolution in India had already taken root. P.V. Narsimha Rao, formed the government at the center in June, 1991 after a period of quick political transactions. Rao choose an experienced economist, Manmohan Singh, as the Finance Ministry, who started a policy of economic reforms. India's entry into the international economic playground caught the imagination of the American Commerce, Treasury and Energy Departments as well as American corporations and business houses.[71] As a part of its economic reforms program, the Rao government abolished equity participation of more than 40% and the provision requiring the use of locally available materials, gave up its strategy of import substitution in favor of exports led growth, removed quantitative restrictions on foreign trade and reduced customs duties on imports.

The Prime Minister also spent much of his time meeting with American businessmen, which according to one source, resulted in agreements on American investment of between $20 and 25$ billion over the next years (it is currently slight over 2$ billion in approved investment). Thus, it is apparent that while the normal lines of diplomatic communication were generating a confusing fog, business channels between New Delhi and Washington emerged as a powerful force for stabilizing relations.[72] According to the data provided by the Indian Embassy, the US is India's largest trading partner and export destination. Two way trades between the two countries totaled almost $13 billion in 1999 and have grown almost 300 percent since 1992. With the exception of India's computer software exports to the US trade between the two countries typifies that between a developing and a developed country. India's exports of items such textiles and apparel, footwear and leather products, cut and polished non-industrial diamonds, carpets, shrimp prawns and cashew nuts account for 75% of the total exports to

---

[71] Ibid. P- 15.

[72] Jha, Nalini Kant n-7. P -1043.

the US. As might be expected, India's imports from the US include Machinery, fertilizers, aircraft and aeronautical equipment and organic chemicals. The table given below gives us an overview of the US Indian bilateral trade.[73]

India-US Bilateral Trade

	1992	1993	1994	1995	1996	1997	1998	1999
Exports % growth	3.781	4.551 +20.44	5.302 +16.5	5.736 +8.2	6.169 +7.5	7.321 +18.7	8.225 +12.3	9.083 +10.4
Imports % growth	1.914	2.761 +44.3	2.296 -16.8	3.296 +43.6	3.318 +0.7	3.616 +9.1	3.545 +2.1	3.707 +4.6
Balance	1.8666	1.790	3.005	2.440	2.851	3.705	4.680	5.376

Source: Embassy of Washington D.C.

Prime Minister Narasimha Rao during his tour to United States in May 1994 sought to convey India's desire to enhance Indo-Us economic co-operation. At first he struck friendly note through his remark that Indo-US relations are on the threshold of a bold new era. We have seen unprecedented co-operation in a number of areas. But, on top of his agenda were the issues where the Countries had not yet worked that closely, namely trade, investment and transfer of technology.[74]This is the evident from the fact that while the US has emerged in India's largest trading partner America share his 20% in India's export-India's

[73] Gandhi ,Prem P. India-US Economic Relations: A Perspective Ed. Kapur, Ashok, Malik,Y.K India and USA in Changing World. New Delhi : Sage Publication, 2002. PP-329, 330.

[74] Chintamani ,Mahapatra. n-2, P- 20.

share in the America can global trade is still less than one percent. Similarly, while only a small fraction of the American global investment in India, the US is the largest foreign investor in this country. The US is also India's largest technology partner. As the trade deficit rose continuously and placed by 1987, this gave room for a strong feeling within the US that the deficit was the result of the unfair practices of its trading partners. This in turn, resulted in increasing demand for protection, congress, which is closer to popular sentiments, supported this demand. That is why, soon after its inauguration, the Clinton administration initiated some protectionist measures. Though India was not affected, yet these moves coupled with talks in the US Congress of reintroducing the 'super 301' legislation. Which allows Washington to impose unilateral sanctions to try open markets, panicked many world capitals including New Delhi.[75]

3.2 Pokhran 2nd and its impact upon Indo-US relation

On 11 May 1998, India donated five nuclear devices at Pokhran, the site of its first nuclear test 24 year earlier. Just two weeks later, Pakistan donated six nuclear devices at the Chagai Hills. These events sharply focused President Clinton and his administrations attention on South Asia.[76]

India's nuclear test in May 1998 angered to Clinton administration, but also provided the shock necessary for a more substantive security dialogue between the two countries.[77] The Prime Minister special Secretary Brajesh Mishra

---

[75] Dilip, M. India USA and the Emerging World Order. Baroda: University of Baroda, 1995. P- 234.

[76] Malone, David M. and Mukherjee, Rohan, "The Shock of the New," Canadian International Journal, Vol. 64, No. 4, (Autumn 2009): Canadian International Council.1063.

[77] Mohan C. Raja. India and the Emerging Non-Proliferation Order: The

said "we remain committed to a truly comprehensive arrangement to prohibit underground testing as well as related experiments described as sub-critical or 'hydro-nuclear' we are for speedy nuclear disarmament. "The tests are not directed at US' as the US would the people of India.[78] But the USA government found the nuclear test by India an insult to the US efforts to prevent nuclear proliferation. The President Bill Clinton stated that he was deeply disturbed by the nuclear tests that he did not believe that such contributed to building a safe 21st Century and added that this action by India not only threatens the stability of the region, it directly challenges the firm international consensus to stop the proliferation of weapons of mass destruction.[79]

US President Bill Clinton after India's nuclear tests in 1988 announced imposition of sanctions against India under section 102 of the US Arms Export Control Act, also known as the Glenn Amendment.[80] The economic sanctions imposed by the United States in response to India's nuclear tests in May 1998 appeared, at least initially, to seriously damage Indo-American relations. President Bill Clinton imposed wide-ranging sanctions pursuant to 1994 Nuclear Proliferation prevention Act US sanctions on Indian entities involved in the nuclear industry and opposition to international financial institution loan for non-humanitarian assistance projects in India. The United States encouraged India to sign the Comprehensive Test Ban Treaty (CTBT) immediately and without condition. The US also called on to restraint in missiles and nuclear testing and deployment by both India and Pakistan. The proliferation dialogue initiated after the 1998 nuclear tests has bridged many of the gaps in understanding between India and United States.[81]

Second Nuclear Age. Ed. Pant, Harsh V. Indian Foreign Policy in a Unipolar World, London: Routledge Publication, 2009.P-62.

[78] Hindustan Times. May 12, 1998.

[79] Chintamani, Mahapatra. n-2, P- 158.

[80] Ibid. P- 158.

3.3 Kashmir Crisis and Indo-US Relation

The Relations between Indo-Pakistan deteriorated in 1990 because of growing incidence of Islamabad militancy in Kashmir; President George Bush sent Deputy National Security Advisor, Robert Gates and Assistant Secretary of the State John Kelly to the subcontinent. It was reported in the American Press that Gates had impressed upon New Delhi and Islamabad that yet another round of war over Kashmir could lead to nuclear confrontation.[82] It is just for this reason that it is not too surprising that the United States raised the question of Kashmir soon after the Indian tests. Since for decades the United States had essentially no useful leverage on the conflict over Kashmir, even a straw might seem worth grasping at.[83]

The US policy towards the Kashmir issue never has been helpful towards resolution of this problem.[84] Some Indians in particular feel that, though Kashmir is a sensitive issue for them, the United States has always tried to take advantage whenever India has been in a weak position- be it food aid in the 1960's need for military assistance during the 1962 Sino-Indian war in 1998's pressure to lift economic sanctions by placing pressure on Kashmir negotiation.[85]

---

[81] Zia, Ahmad Rakib. n-12, P- 317.

[82] Chintammani, Mahapatra. n-2, P- 44.

[83] Clifford E. Singer, Jyotika, Saksena. "Feasible Deals With India and Pakistan After The Nuclear Tests; The Glenn Sanctions and US Negotiations," Asian Survey, Vol. 38, No.12, Dec (1 998): 1170.

[84] Chintamani, Mahapatra. n-2, P- 45.

[85] Clifford, E.Singer. n-26, P-1172.

CHAPTER 4TH

Indo-American Relations in 21st Century

(2000-2004)

The Vajpayee government tried to build on the foundations laid by the Narsimha Rao government of a new foreign policy based on establishment of good relations with the west. Developing stable, normal relations with the US remained a very important objective of its foreign policy. There was a considerable increase in bilateral dialogue between the two democracies during the period between January and March2000. The dialogue on Non-Proliferation, security and disarmament, which was resumed in London in November 1999, was further continued from January 18-19, 2000 in London. Besides this two nations also had extensive discussions on counter-terrorism, the hijacking of the Indian Airlines, Air craftIC-814, regional developments and President Clinton's visit to India. India and America at London announced the formation of Indo-US joint working group on counter-terrorism, which held its first meeting from February 7-82000 in

Washington D.C.[86] On 21-25 March 2000, Clinton became the first US President to visit India in 22 years.[87] While he reached out to the Indian people and successfully removed much of the accumulated poison in bilateral relations, he was not prepared to put the future of the relationship with India above his administration's non-proliferation goals until the last day, Clinton officials insisted that the full potential of Indo-U.S relations cannot be realized without India meeting the benchmarks, especially the CTBT. The Clinton administration was unwilling to elevate the bilateral relationship above the presumed imperatives of the US non-proliferation policy.[88]

During the visit of President Clinton to Delhi in March 2000, Prime Minister Vajpayee and President Clinton agreed as a part of their vision for the future relationship that regular, wide ranging dialogue is important for achieving the goal of establishing closer and multifaceted relations between the India and the United States and for the two countries to work jointly for the promotion of peace and prosperity in the 21st century. The President also invited the Prime Minister to visit USA and the later accepted the invitation.[89] The President Bill Clinton addressed a joint session of the Indian Parliament.[90] In a joint statement with Indian Prime Minister Atal Bihari Vajpayee in New Delhi, President Clinton

---

[86] Shukla, S. Foreign Policy Of India. New Delh: Anamika Publishers, 2007.PP-250,253.

[87] Malone, David M. and Mukherjee, Rohan. "India US Relations: The Shock Of The New", International Journal, Vol. 64, No. 4, Autum (2009):1064.

[88] Mohan,.C. Raja. India and The Emerging Non Proliferation Order: The Second Nuclear Age. Pant Harsh V. Indian Foreign Policy In a Unipolar World. New Delhi: Routledge Publication, 2009, P-63.

[89] URL/www.acronym.org.UK/spvisit. Html acessed on 06-04-2014.

[90] Ibid.

[91] Ramtanu Maitra 'Clinton and Vajpayee move to strengthen indo American relation.EIR Volume 27, No. 14, April 7, (2000):51.

said: "I have come to India because I want to build a dynamitic and lasting partnership, based on mutual benefit. [91]

Vajpayee and Bill Clinton signed the five page "vision for the 21st century" that affirmed both leaders resolve to "create closer and qualitatively new relationship". The statement reviewed the two side's differences over non-proliferation and committed the governments to institutionalize the dialogue.[92]

September 2000, Shri Atal Bihari Vajpaye visited the United States. Though the tour had several other engagements the last phase was exclusively devoted to building Indo-US relation. During the visit, a few agreements were signed, formal speeches made, informal and formal statements were issued by authorities of both countries, press conferences were held and interviews were given. All these help in gaining some insight into the emerging Indo-US relation.

During the visit of Prime Minister Vajpayee to the U.S, he was given the honor of being the only foreign leader to address the joint sitting of the 106th session of the US Congress. He was welcomed there by a resolution adopted by House of Representatives and the senate, which called for building stronger Indo-US relation. He had restricted and a high level delegation meeting with President Clinton and the Vice President Al. Gore. President Clinton relation would become one of the important factors in international affairs in the future. The two sides reaffirmed their view that the tension in South Asia can only be resolved by the nations of South Asia and by peaceful means.[93] During the new Bush administration Indo-US relations have developed at a peace that few could have for seen. In this confirmation hearings before the senate Foreign Relations Committee, the then secretary of State designate Colin Powell stated, India has the

---

[92] D. Sivakumar. "Indo-US Relations during The NDA Regime." Third Concept, Vol. 23. No. 271, Sep. (2009):22.

[93] URL/www.idsa-India.org/an-de-00-8.html/ acessed on 06-04-2014.

potential to help keep the peace in the vast Indian Ocean area and its periphery. We need to work harder and more consistently to help them in this endeavor.[94]

Prior to the terrorist attacks of September 2001, the wheels of the US Indian relationship were thus steadily, even though gradually, in motion. The incoming Bush administration further energized Clinton's pro-Indian policies. When Indian External Affairs Minister Jaswant Singh met with National Security Advisor Condoleeza Rice in April 2001, President George W. Bush met informally with Singh in the oval office, a gesture most welcome by New Delhi. The next month, Deputy Secretary of State Richard Armitage made a stop in India to garner approval for Bush administration controversial missile defense plans. Instead of seizing upon an opportunity to publicly criticize Washington for its perceived hypocrisy with regard to relevant international agreements, Singh welcomed the policy and contended that the two countries were "endeavoring to work out together a totally new security regime which is for the entire globe," a notion heretofore unimaginable in the context of the US-India relationship. While many US allies criticized America's missile defense policy, India conspicuously, if only rhetorically, stood by Washington's side.[95]

During 2001 the joint military exercises were resumed. These had earlier been mainly confined to naval exercises since1992, but were now extended to land and air exercises. When Bush announced his National Missile Defense Program, India became the first country to welcome it.[96] The September 11, 2001 attacks in the US came as an unexpected setback to the plan of the BJP government. Vajpayee immediately wrote to President Bush offering to be a partner in the war

[94] Shukla, S, n-1, PP- 254, 255.

[95] htpp/www.Ph.gov.av/About/PalimentaryLibrary/Pubs/rp/rp0102/02rp20/ acessed on 09-04-2014.

[96] K. Alan Kronstadt. January 24, 2013. "U.S-India Security Relations, Strategic Issues." CRS Report for Congress. P-3.

against terrorism and placing India's military facilities at the disposal. The BJP leadership could not hide their disappointment when the US choose Pakistan as the frontline state in the war against Afghanistan a fact that Advani sorrowfully called the logic 'logic of geography' this however, only added to the determination of the Vajpayee government to convince the US of its credentials to be a natural ally. L.K. Advani as the Dy. Prime Minister visited Washington. To make sure that their message went home, Advani visited the CIA headquarters to meet the director of the CIA to talk of security co-operation against terrorism. The FBI was allowed to open an office in Delhi.[97]

By 22 September, the US had lifted all sanctions against India and the bilateral defense policy of group, suspended since 1998, was revived towards the end of the year. Following a terrorist attack on the Indian parliament in December 2001, the US pressured Pakistan into a commitment on curbing cross border terrorism in India.[98] It was the first time in September 2003, the Bush administration put India in the category of great powers and according to C. Raja Mohan (crossing the Rubicon), and the US "suggested an Indian role in Asian balance of power and contrasted a positive approach towards India with a more critical one toward China." The change in the US-India relations was based on the conviction that the US interest required a strong relationship with India. Thus US Ambassador to India Robert Black will declared in late 2002 that, peace with in Asia was an objective that a transformed US- India relationship would help advance. Thus, both India and the United States began working to strengthen their relationship in various spheres. As ambassador Black will said, a strong US-India partnership contributing to the construction of a peaceful and prosperous Asia binds the resources of the world's most powerful and most populous

[97] Karat, Prakash. "Subordinate Ally: Implications of The Indo-US Strategic Alliance." The Marxist, Vol. XXII. No. 1, January- March, (2001):2.

[98] Malon, David M. and Mukherjee, Rohan. "India US Relations: The Shock of the New. "International journal," Vol. 64. No. 4, Autumn (2009):1064.

democracies in support of freedom, poetical moderation, and economic and technological development.[99]

With the war against terrorism declared, the document reiterates that pre-emptive military action is required to prevent hostile action by adversaries. For this the US will require bases and military stations outside Western Europe and Northeast Asia, as well as temporary access arrangement for the long distance deployment of US forces. The Pentagon had commissioned a study by one of the think tanks affiliated to it. The Report was called to the India-US military Relationship; Expectations and perceptions" and came out in October 2002. Forty Serving senior U.S officials were interviewed for the study. Among the observations were the Indian armed forces could be used "for low-end operations in Asia such as peace keeping operations, search and rescue.[100]In 2003, the US invaded Iraq under the pretext of the mass weapons after UNO's inspection. Sadam Hussain tried to retaliate but failed in his attempt to face the US-led coalition forces.[101]

However, the two countries held different views on the question of military action against Iraq in the summer of 2003, India, like Russia, France and Germany was against any action without authorization by the UN Security Council. Despite opposition by several countries, the US President Bush and British Prime Minister Tony Blair went ahead with their military operations in which President Saddam Husain was ousted, later captured and finally hanged. They failed to recover any alleged weapons of mass destruction.[102] The USA asked Indian government for the military help to restore the Iraq. Foreign Secretary of

---

[99] Khanna V .N. Foreign Policy of India. New Delhi: Vikas Publication, P-280.

[100] Karat Prakash, n-12, P-3.

[101] Siva Kumar. D,N. "Indo-US Relations in Perspective." Third Concept, Vol. 23 No. 270, August, 2009. P- 37.

[102] Khanna VN. n-14, P- 282.

India, Kawal Sibl, visited to Washington. At the Pentagon the US Deputy Secretary of Defense Paul Wolfowitz, was reported to have told Sibal that the Indian forces might be required for as long as 30 months. The Indian force was required by the US command to be in the Kurd-controlled northern part of Iraq.[103]

Vajpayee government refused to lend Indian troops to Iraq.[104] Indian hesitation to join the U.S. in its Iraq vent lire has indeed exposed the underlying differences in the way the two nations define terrorism and the most effective means to combat it. The refusal to send Indian troops was publicly attributed to a number of factors. The lack of a United Nations mandate, domestic political opposition and finally, the need for Indian troops in Kashmir. The United States had apparently wanted India to deploy a division-15,000 to 20,000 soldiers – but in July 2003, India turned Washington's request citing the absence of a UN mandate. Another reason cited later was the clear domestic opposition to such a move. It was not lost on observers that national elections were at the time slated to be held by October 2004, and that two ruling party would pay a high political cost if any soldier died in Iraq. In September 2003, it was reported that U.S. assistant secretary of state for south Asia Chsistina Rocca raised the issue of troops again in New Delhi. This time around India apparently argued that its troops were too tied up fighting militancy in Kashmir.[105]

While the US state department in its reaction on July 2003, expressed that the U.S. a hoped India would have made a different choice, that they would have been there, it also reiterated that India remained an important strategic partner for the united states, and that the continuation of the transformation of Indo-US relations was something that was important to them. In recognition of India's

---

[103] Siva Kumar D. "Sending Indian troops to Iraq and Indo-US Relations." "Third Concept, Vol. 24. No. 285, November (2010): 37.

[104] Sivakumar D. n-16, P- 37.

[105] Htpp/www.gwu.rdu/sigur/assets/docs/scap/scap22-Ollapally. Pdf.

concerns, the U.S. secretary of state, Colin Powell, said in an interview on 22 September 2003, that though India had a large standing body of troops, it was, probably, politically too difficult for India to send any troops to Iraq, India's potential for contribution to the post war reconstruction and development efforts in Iraq is recognized.[106]

4.1 U.S-INDIA ECONOMIC DIALOGUE

In order to take the process of cooperation forward and to widen its scope, President Bush and Indian Prime Minister Atal Bihari Vajpaye announced next steps strategic partnership (NSPP). In January 2004 which turned out to be a milestone in emerging Indo-Us relations. Under NSSP, both the sides agreed to take reciprocal measures to facilitate cooperation in technology transfer. U.S agreed to ease restrictions on the transfer of technology to India in three important areas, civil nuclear technology, civil space and the dual use of technology goods.[107] The next steps strategic partnership first phase was concluded in September 2004 when Indian Foreign Secretary Shyan Sasan and U.S undersecretary of state Kenneth Juster sealed an agreement under which Indian Space Research Organization (ISRO) was removed from entity list and license requirements for exporting low level dual use items to Indian research organizations were also eased.[108]

---

[106] Shukla, S. n-1, PP- 260, 261.

[107] Rai,K.Ajai. India's Nuclear Diplomacy After Pokhran II. New Delhi : Darling Kindersley, 2009. P-22.

[108] Mistry,Dinshaw. " Diplomacy Domestic Politics and US-Indian Nuclear Agreement." "Asian Survey, Vol. 46. No.5, September-October, (2006):681,682.

During the visit of US President Clinton to India in March 2000, a joint statement on "US-India Relations:- A version for the 21ist century" was issued by the Prime Minister Vajpayee and President Clinton which pledged to deepen the Indo-American partnership through dialogue and engagement. It also outlined an architecture of several high level consultations which would institutionalize this dialogue in a separate document" Agreed principles: institutional dialogue between the United States and India." This architecture laid out the following frame work for the bilateral economic dialogue.

High level coordinating group led on Indian side by Deputy Chairman Planning Commission with Ministry of External Affairs support led on US side by white House with states Department support. The agreed principles provided for (a) setting up a joint consultative group of clean energy and environment and (b) establishing US-India science and Technology forum, both of which were strictly not under the fabric of economic dialogues.

Besides this in 2001 two more additional forum were created to address environment and energy issues under the economic dialogue. Following meetings at the level of Prime Minister Vajpayee and President Bush in November 2002, efforts began to develop a "Statement of Principles" on High Technology trade including trade in "dual use" goods and technologies. On February 5, 2003 a "Statement of principles for India US High Technology Commerce" was signed in Washington DC.[109]

4.2 TRADE RELATIONS

---

[109] Syed, H Muzaffar. Indo-US Relations. New Delhi: Orange Books International, 2012. P- 54.

During the Bush administration, trade relations with India increased dramatically comparable to previous years. As per US trade data released by the US department of commerce, worldwide merchandise exports to US grew during calendar year 2002 by+1.98 percent. Out of top 25 exporting countries to the US, growth rates for 14 were positive, while 11 countries witnessed steep decline in their exports to US.

Merchandise exports from India to US grew by + 21.4 percent in 2002 by compared to 2001, rising from $ 9.74 billion to 4 11.82 billion. The good news in terms of US-India trade relations was that India had emerged as the 19th largest merchandise exporter to US in 2002 with a 1.02 percent share of total US imports up from a 0.86% share in 2001, 2002 marks the first year that India had entered the list of top 20 countries exporting to US, it was also the first time that India's exports to the US had exceeded 1% of US merchandise imports. It also marked the first time in recent years that the ratio of growth of Indian merchandise exports to US (21.45) had outpaced the rate of growth in our India's services exports to US (20%).

Growth had been more or less across the board and major Indian export growth sectors in 2002 included diamonds, gold jewelers (+39%), woven apparel (+9%), linen and other textile items (+23%), Knit apparel (+13%), fish and sea food (+36%), carpets (+19%), machinery (+23%), iron and steel (+270%) and pharmaceuticals (+136).[110]

Us exports to India, which remained flat for a long a period, increased by 19% in 2003 when they crossed RS. 18, 400 crore ($4 billion), for the first time. In 2003, US exports to India increased on a year-on-year basis by over 18% to RS. 20, 240 crore ($4.4 billion). While US imports from India rose by 11% to over RS

---

[110] Alam, Badrul .Mohammad. Indo-US Relations: Dimensions and Emerging Trends. New Delhi: Shipra Publications, 2013.PP-4, 5.

59, 800 crore ($13 billion) US Deputy Secretary of commerce Samuel W. Bodman was quick to acknowledge the change when he came to New Delhi in early 2003 sating, "A year ago I lamented the low levels of U.S exports and FDI into India. This year I can export some good news.[111]

---

[111] Please See. "People Progress, Partnership: The Transformation Of US-India Relation" New Delhi Printed and Published by The Public Affairs Section Of The Embassy Of the USA, 2003, PP-25, 26.

Chapter 5th

INDO-AMERICAN RELATION DURING UPA- I

(2004-2009)

The NDA government led by Atal Bihari Vajpayee completed five years of term of rule in 2004. Subsequently the 14th general election of India was held in 2004. The congress was able to manage a majority of more than 335 seats out of 543. The United Progressive alliance first (UPA-I) was formed with the help of the BSP, SP, DMK, and left front under the Prime ministership of Dr. Manmohan Singh in 2004.[112] The UPA government has taken major steps to convert India into ally of U.S.A. This is meaning of a strategic partnership which has been forged between the two countries. If there were any doubts on the American side, that this change over would lead to an interruption of the process, they were quickly dispelled. Even though the common minimum program scrupulously avoids any reference to strategic relations with the US, events seen proved that this was the way maters were heading. The joint working groups, the negotiations on the next steps in strategic partnership, the defense policy group, all began meeting it as a business usual.

The omission of a strategic relationship with the US in the CMP was made up in the first presidential address to parliament in June 2004, where it was stated that a closer "strategic and economic engagement with the US will be pursued.[113]

---

[112] Badal Sarkar. "India's Foreign Policy Under the Prime Minister of Dr. Manmohan Singh," International Journal of Scientific Research, Vol. 2, No. 12, December, (2013):514.

[113] Karat Prakash."Subordinate Ally: Implications of the Indo-US Strategic Alliance." The Marxist, Vol. XXII, No. I, January-March, 2006 .PP-1-4.

The visit of Condoleezza Rice in March in 2005 proved to be a significant turning point. Rice had taken over as a secretary of the state in the second Bush term which began in January 2005. Rice declared that the US was prepared to "help" India for becoming a "great power". In second phase of the Bush presidency, the US began the rhetoric of addressing India's great power aspirations.[114]

5.1 DEFENCE PARTNERSHIP.

The visit of Condoleezza Rice set the stage for the UPA government's invitation into the big game already in play with the BJP-led government. The Indian defense Minister's visit to Washington in June brought this out graphically. Pranab Mukherjee innocuously announced to the media that it was "an exploratory visit." Such exploration yielded something very substantial, in the form of ten year Defense Frame work Agreement.[115] India's defense and security cooperation with the United States has also made significant progress over the last decade. While growth has been largely incremental reflected in the sophistication of exercises and intensity of mil-to-mil cooperation. The conclusion of the new frame work for the India-US Defense Relationship on 28 June 2005 marked a quantum change. This framework articulated the shared security and stability, defeating terrorism and violent religious extremism, and protecting the free flow of commerce via land, air and sea lanes. To that end, it was agreed that Indian and US defense forces would conduct joint and combined exercises and exchanges, collaborate in multinational operation when it is in their common interest, strengthen military capabilities including in counter terrorism, expand the defense trade, provide for technology transfers, collaborations, co-production and R and

---

[114] Ibid, P- 4.

[115] Karat, Prakash. n-2, P- 5.

D and exchange intelligence. A new defense procurement and production groups were constituted to oversee defense trade, coproduction and technology collaboration. Consequent to this new frame work, a Disaster relief initiative was finalized in July 2005 and a maritime Cooperation Frame work in March 2006.[116]

The India US joint declaration, issued by Prime Minister Manmohan Singh and President George W Bush in March 2006, welcomed increased bilateral cooperation in the defense area under the new frame work, evidenced by successful joint exercises, information sharing and greater opportunities to jointly develop technologies and security and humanitarian issues. The dialogue between the two countries on defense co-operation related issues has been ongoing. It received further directions and impetus with visit of US Secretary of Defense Robert Gates to India on February 26-7-2008 and the visit of India's Defense Minister to US from September 7-10-2008 at the invitation of secretary Robert Gates.[117]

In 2006, India brought the US Trenton, a decommissioned American Amphibious Transport dock for $ 44 million. This was later named the INS Salashwa. Subsequent India spent another $ 39 million on sikorsky UH-3H to buy six C-130j Hercules military transport aircrafts worth nearly $ 1 billion from the US. In 2009, it agreed to buy eight P-81 maritime surveillance aircraft, worth $ 1 billion, six c-1301j transport aircraft worth $ 1 billion and 99 jet engines for the Tejas LCA worth around $800 from general Electric.[118]

---

[116] Jaim, Shankar.S. India and USA: new directions. Ed. Sinha, Atish and Mohta Mahup. Indian Foreign Policy: Challenges and Opportunities. New Delhi: Academic Foundation, 2007. P-785.

[117] Syed, Muzzafar H. Indo-US Relations. New Delhi: Orange Books, 2012. P-66.

[118] Purushothaman, Uma. Indo-US Defense Relations: Challenges and Prospects. Ed. Alam Badrul

Mohammad. <u>Indo-US Relations: Dimensions, and Emerging Trends</u>. New Delhi: Shipra

Publication, 2013. PP- 31, 32.

[119] http:/www.dsca.mil/programmes/biz-ops/facyts-book/fiscal   year   series-2010 Pdf, accessed on

28.04.2014.

The table shows USA Military Assistance and Sales to India From 2004-2009.[119]

Years	Total Sales Agreement	Total Sales Deliveries	FMS Agreements	FMS Deliveries	Foreign Mil Fin Waived	Foreign Min Fin Direct	Commercial Export Deliveries
2004	946	6, 567	946	6, 567	-	-	15, 516
2005	76, 885	100, 328	76, 885	100, 328	-	-	31, 891
2006	25	48, 576	25	48, 576	-	-	39, 673
2007	92, 340	91, 999	92, 340	91, 999	-	-	27, 784
2008	1,020,944	40, 148	1, 20, 944	40, 108	-	-	129, 516
2009	10, 401	15,004	10, 401	15, 004	-	-	-
Total	1,201,541	302,582	1, 201541	302,582	0	0	244, 380

This table shows the US Arms sales to India.[120]

NO. ORDERED	WEAPON DESIGNATION	WEAPON DESCRIPTION	YEAR. OF ORDER/ LICENSE	YEAR OF DELIVERIES	NO. DELIVERED PRODUCED	COMMENTS
17	F-404	TURBOFAN	2004			F 404-GE-1N20 Version, ordered after India Kavery Engine delayed. EX-US, INR2.2B($48 Million) deal (including modernization) Indian Designation
1	AUSTIN S-61/H-3A SEA	AALS	2006	2007	1	Jalashwa EX-US, 39 Million $, UH-3H Version #100 Million deal, for Tejas (LCA) Combat Aircraft produced in India

[120] Purushothaman, Uma. n-7, P- 41.

6	KING	HELICO PTER	2006	2007	6	F-404 GE-F2J3 Version $1 Billion deal (included $ 596 Million for aircraft and $ 400 Million for special equipment), C-130J-30 Version for special for us.
24	F-404	TURBOF AN	2007			
6	HERCUL ES-2C-17A	AIRCRA FT	2008	2010	1	

5.2 JOINT MILITARY EXERCISES.

Interoperability is a key aim of the Indo-US defiance relationship. This is possible only when the armed forces of both countries are familiar with each other's producers, system and methodologies and when there is trust between them. Interoperability also depends on compatibility of equipment. Joint exercises are one way of enhancing interoperability. They are therefore the key component of Indo-US defense relations. The Indian and American navies conduct three joint exercises annually i.e., Habu Nag (naval aspects of amphibious operations.) Splitting Cobra (explosive ordnance destruction focus), and Salvex (diving and

Salvage).[121] Moreover, the Indian and American navies have cooperated operationally on four separate occasions: security by the Indian Navy for US ship transiting the Strait of Malacca after 9/11, disaster relief effort after the Indian Ocean tsunami in 2004-2005, non-combatant evacuation operations in Lebanon in 2006 and counter piracy operations in the Gulf of Aden sinle 2008.[122]

The US and Indian Armies have been conducting Yudha Abhyas exercise annually since from 2004. This was the first conventional army to army training in India since 1962. In 2005, U.S troops came to train at India's counter insurgency and jungle warfare school. In 2006, Indian troops went to Hawaii for training and in 2007, troops travelled to Alaska. The Lt. Gen. Benjamin R. Mixon said, "We want to be able to work together as militaries. By US training together and getting to know each other, if there were a contingency, we should be better prepare to respond to that contingency. You can't do that training here at the last minute."[123]

The Indian air force participated in the multinational air exercise" Exercise Red Flag" at the Nellis AFB, USA in August 2008. IAF's participation included eight SU-30s and two IL-78 air-to-air refueled aircraft one IL-76 transport aircraft and a ten member GAURO team. The contingent comprised a total of 247 personnel.[124]

---

[121] Syed, Muzaffer H. n-6, P- 32.

[122] Report to Congress On USIndian Security Cooperation, US Department of Defense Nov.2011,http;/www.defense.gov/pubs/pdfs/20/11/2001-NDA-Report on US-Indian-Security-Cooperation.pdf, P-4, Accessed on 27, 4, 2014.

[123] U.S –Indian Armies wrap up historic exercises by Fred W.Barker III Oct.]2009, Avilable on

http:/www.army.mil/article/29473/UD Indian armies wrap up.historic exercise /carnegieedowment.org/relations....g18......accessed on 04-05-2014

[124] Syed, Muzaffer H. n-6, P- 68.

5.3 INDO-U.S CIVIL NUCLEAR DEAL.

The agreement signed between the United States of America and the Republic of India is known as the US-India Civil Nuclear Agreement or Indo-US nuclear deal.[125]

The deal, an offer to India for civil nuclear energy cooperation from the US, was born in George Bush's second presidential term in 2005, after Condoleezza Rice became the new US Secretary of State.[126] During visit Rice expressed the willingness of Bush administration to cooperate with India in the field of civil nuclear energy. Indians were highly surprised by this offer and lost no time in seizing the opportunity and immediately after her visit, the two sides started negotiations to chalk out contours for this broad cooperation.[127] Prime Minister Manmohan Singh paid a land mark July 2005 visit to Washington, where what may be most significant joint US-India statement to date was issued.[128] During his visit, the Bush administration declared its ambition to achieve full civil nuclear energy cooperation with India as part of its broader goals of promoting nuclear power and achieving nuclear security. Both President Bush and Prime Minister Manmohan Singh issued a joint statement on 18 July 2005, which set a framework for Indo-US-Civil Nuclear agreement. In the joint statement President Bush described India as a responsible state with highly advanced nuclear related technology and stated that it "should acquire same benefits and advantages as other states". The Bush administration also to seek agreement from congress to

---

[125] Syed, Muzaffer H. n-6,P- 83.

[126] Aiyar, Vidya Shankar. Prime Time Deal. Ed., Chari P.R. Indo-US Nuclear Deal, Seeking Synergy in Bilateralism. New Delhi: Routledge, P- 82.

[127] Ganaie, Muzzafar Ahmad. Indo U.S Civil Nuclear Deal: Heralding a New Era in Indo-U.S Relations. Ed. Alam Mohammad Badrul. Indo-U.S relations: Dimensions and Emerging Trends. New Delh: Shipra Publication, 2013. P-49.

[128] Http://www.Whitehouse.gov/news/releases/2005/07/200050718-6.html/. Acessed on 03-05- 2014.

adjust US laws and policies to work with friends and allies to adjust international regimes to enable full civil nuclear energy cooperation and trade with in India.[129] Indian Prime Minister Dr. Manmohan Singh in response stated that India would assume the same responsibilities and safety, practices and derive the amen benefits and advantages as other leading countries and would work towards.[130]

- Splitting its nuclear facilities into military and civil ones and placing the later under international Atomic Energy Agency.
- Continuing its unilateral moratorium on nuclear testing.
- Early conclusion of Fissile material cut of treaty.
- Ensuring strict control on the transfer of sensitive nuclear technology to states that do not have such technology.

After the July 18, 2005 statement, India started negotiations with US interlocutors to split its nuclear facilities into civil and military ones called "separation plan" US position on this plan was clear that it should be very comprehensive from non-proliferation stand point and Bush urged India "to produce a credible, transparent and defensible plan to separate its civilian and military nuclear programs under the same international safeguards that govern nuclear powered programs in other countries.[131] On March 3, 2006, President George Bush's visit to India proved significant for both India and U.S.A which marked a new phase between them. It was during this visit the two countries finally managed to reach a crucial understanding on the separation plan for India's nuclear facilities, the first step towards putting the July 2005 agreement into effect.[132] The Indian plan to separate

---

[129] Joint Statement Between President George w. Bush and Prime Minister Mamohan Singh, 18 july 2005, available at URL: http://www.George w. Bush-white house. Archives.gov./news/releases/2005/07/20050718-6.html/ acessed on 04-05-2014.

[130] Ibid.

[131] Ganie, Muzzafar Ahmad. n-16, P- 50.

[132] U.S Indian Joint Statement March 2006, available at Url:Http://www. George Bush.White HouseArchives.gov/news/releases/2006/03120060302-5

civilian and weapons reactors facilities met the United States bench makers of being creditable, verifiable and defensible from the non-proliferation standpoint. The main points of the deal were:-

- India's 14 thermal reactors out of 22 reactors are to be separated as civilian and placed under International Atomic Energy Agency (IAEA) safe guards.

- The reactors once safeguarded under IAEA will remain permanently in its observation. Indian secures to right to take corrective action if the reactor fuel supply is stopped.

- It will depend upon India whether it wishes to safeguard the future reactors.

- Enrichment and reprocessing plants can switch back and forth from safeguards, depending upon whether they handed safeguarded material or not.

- The nuclear separation would be done in phases but will be concluded by 2014.[133]

To ally doubts and suspicions about the separation agreement, the Prime Minister has repeatedly made detailed statements that India's strategic program will not be adversely affected, that India will not cease the production of Fissile material for weapons purpose ahead of a Fissile Material Test Ban Treaty (FMCT) being negotiated and that India reserved its right to conduct further nuclear tests if circumstances so warranted-in other words, the present moratorium on nuclear testing will not become an absolute prohibition.[134]

---

html, accessed on 05-05-2014.

[133] Gupta, K.R. Indo-U.S Nuclear Cooperation. Ed. Bhonsle, Rahul Prakash Ved and Gupta,
    R, K, S. Indo-U.S Nuclear Deal, Vol. 1. (2007):148.

[134] Chari P.R. Introduction: The Indo-U.S Nuclear Deal. Ed, Chari P.R. Indo-U.S Nuclear Deal Seeking Synergy in Bilateralism. New Delhi: Routledge Publisher, 2009.P-15.

After separation plan was finalized, Bush administration passed Henry J. Hyde United State-India peaceful Atomic Energy Cooperation Act also called Hyde Act after the name of outgoing chairman of House International Relations Committee Henry J. Hyde on 18, December, 2006. The Act provides legal basis for nuclear cooperation between India and United States. It was necessary for Bush administration to pass this act as it waives some of the requirements of US Atomic Energy Act of 1954. These requirements are:-

- A country should have full scope safeguards in place.

- A country should not have exploded a nuclear device in past (after March 10, 1978).

- A country should not be involved in activities leading to the production of nuclear explosive devices.

A country is eligible for nuclear cooperation with U.S, Only if it fulfills these requirements. As India did not fulfill any of these requirements, So Hyde Act was passed which waived these requirements and there by allowed US to engage India in Civil Nuclear Energy Cooperation.[135]

The 123 Agreement crossed the International Atomic Energy Agency hurdle without much difficulty. A proposal for amending the nuclear supply Group (NSG) guidelines were drafted by the United States approved by India and placed before the nuclear supply group committee. The International Atomic Energy (IAEA) Board of Governors and 45 state nuclear suppliers group approved the safeguard agreement on August 1, 2008. The US President George Bush made the necessary certifications and then sought the final approval of the US Congress.[136] On August 1, 2008, the International Atomic Energy Agency

---

[135] Ganaie, Muzaffar Ahmad. n-16, PP-50, 51.

[136] Purushathaman. D. India's 123 Nuclear Agreement With the U.S. Ed., Pilali, Manmohan. B And Premashekhra. L. Foreign Policy of India Continuity and Change. New Delhi: New Century, 2010. P-368.

(IAEA) approved the safeguards agreement with India after which the United States approached the nuclear supplier Group (NSG) to grant a waiver to India to Commence Civilian Nuclear trade. The 45-nation NSG granted the waiver to India on September 06, 2008 allowing it to access civilian nuclear technology and fuel from other countries.[137] The implementation of this waiver made India the only known country with nuclear weapons which is not a party to the Non-proliferation Treaty (NPT) but is still allowed to carry out nuclear commerce with the rest of the world. The US House of Representatives passed the bill on 28 Sep. 2008. Two days later, India and France inked a similar pact making France the first country to have such an agreement with India. On October 1, 2008 the U.S senate also approved the civilian nuclear agreement allowing India to purchase nuclear fuel from the United States. U.S President, George W. Bush, signed the legislation on the Indo- U.S nuclear deal, approved by Congress into law now called the United States India Nuclear Cooperation Approval and Non-Proliferation Enhancement Act, on October 8, 2008.[138]

India and United States on October 10 signed 123 Civil Nuclear Agreement after over three years of intense diplomatic and political discussions a historic move that will restore civil nuclear trade and transform ties between the two countries. This land mark deal will allow India to access to nuclear reactors fuel and technologies from the U.S after the gap of 34 years. Indian's External Affairs Minister Pranab Mukherjeee and U.S Secretary of the state Condoleezza Rice inked the bilateral 123 Agreement at an elegant ceremony in the Benjamin Franklin Room of the State Department. Mukherjee called it "an important day for India- Us relations"." Describing the agreement as, "one more visible sign of the transformed relationship and partnership that our two countries are building together," Mukherjee also said, that in inking the accord "we implement the vision

---

[137] Yadav Surya and Narain Yadav. India's Nuclear Policy: Compulsions, Commitments and Constraints. New Delhi: Jnanda Prakash, 2009.P-78.

[138] Syed, Muzaffar,H. n-16, P- 84.

and understanding reached in July 2005 and March 2006 by the President George Bush and Prime Minister Manmohan Singh."[139]

5.4 OPPOSITION TO THE INDO-US CIVIL NUCLEAR AGREEMENT IN INDIA

In any moment of decision said Theodore Roosevelt, "The best thing you can do is the right thing, the next best thing is the wrong thing, and the worst thing you can do is nothing." After a three year plus debate on the rights and the wrongs, or the 'lefts' and the 'rights' of the deal , the corner stone of India-US relations i.e. The Indo US Civilian Nuclear Agreement was approved by the US senate on 1 October 2008. Finally the agreement was signed on 10 October 2008. As a dust gradually settles on one of India's most controversial achievements in foreign policy, never before has any international issue ignited a debate so extensive where the contention had largely been 'sovereignty' and 'national interest' centric, rather than on the actual agreement. Besides, it is for the first time that a bilateral agreement faced stiff political opposition from both the Indian left and the right.[140] The Indo-US civilian Nuclear Agreement was also opposed by some political parties and activists in India. Although many mainstream political parties including the Indian National Congress support the deal along with regional parties like Dravida Kazhagam and Rashtriya Janata Dal,

---

[139] India, United States Sign historic Civil Nuclear Agreement available at https//www. Indian Embassy. Org/India----/.-

[140] Chakravarthi, Rekh. Internal Road blocks to the Indo-US Nuclear Deal. Ed. Chari.R. Indo-U.S Nuclear Deal: Seeking Synergy in Bilateralism. New Delhi: Routledge Publisher,2009. P- 60.

its realization has run into difficulties in the face of stiff political opposition in India. Also, in November 2007, Former Indian Military Chiefs, bureaucrats and scientists drafted a letter to members of parliament expressing their support for the deal. However, opposition and criticism continued at political levels. The Samajwadi party (SP) which was with the left front in opposing the deal changed its stand after discussing with ex-presidents of India and scientist Dr. A.P.J Abdul Kalam. The Samajwadi party then supported the government and the deal. The Indian government survived a vote of confidence by 275-256 after the left front withdrew their support to the government over this dispute.[141]

The United Nationalist Progressive Alliance (UNPA) was divided over support of the nuclear deal. While the Samajwadi party supported it after consultations with the former President APJ Abdul Kalam the other members of the UNPA led by the Telgu Desam Party (TDP) opposed it. The SP was eventually suspended from the UNPA. The main opposition party Bhartiya Janta Party (BJP) which laid the groundwork for the deal criticized the deal in its present form was unacceptable to the BJP and wanted the deal renegotiated. The BJP had asked the government not to accept the deal without a vote in the parliament. The primary opposition to the nuclear deal in India, however, came from the communist party of India, Revolutionary Socialist Party (India), All India forward Bloc. The left parties had provisionally agreed to let the government initiate talks with the IAEA for India specific safeguards which indicated that they may support. The Bahujan Samaj Party (BSP) also opposed the nuclear deal. The party joined hands with the Left Front and the TDP in voting against the government in parliament on the nuclear deal.[142]

---

[141] India United States Civil Nuclear Agreement available at//en.m.wikipedia.org/wiki/India- United-States-Civil-Nuclear-Agreement.
[142] Syed, Muzaffar.H. n-16, PP- 99,100.

5.5 CHRONOLGY OF INDO-U.S NUCLEAR DEAL.

Following is the chronology of events in the landmark Indo-U.S nuclear agreement since U.S President George Bush and Prime Minister Manmohan Singh conceived the deal in July 2005.

- July 18, 2005: President Bush and Prime Minister Singh first announce their intention to enter a nuclear agreement in Washington.

- March 1, 2006: Bush visits India for the first time. March 3, 2006 Bush and Singh issue a joint statement on their growing strategic partnership, emphasizing their agreement on civil nuclear cooperation.

- July 26, 2006: The US House of Representatives passes the 'Henry J Hyde United States-India Peaceful Atomic Energy Cooperation Act of 2006, which stipulates that Washington will cooperate with New Delhi on nuclear issues and exempt it from signing the Nuclear Non-Proliferation Treaty.

- July 28, 2006: The left parties demand threads bare discussion on the issue in Parliament.[143]

- November 16, 2006: The Senate passes the 'United States-India peaceful Atomic Energy Cooperation and U.S additional protocol implementation Act' to "exempt from certain requirements of the Atomic energy Act of 1954 United States exports of nuclear materials, equipment and technology to India".

- December 18, 2006: President Bush signs into law congressional legislation on Indian atomic energy.

- July 17-20, 2007: Undersecretary of state for Political Affairs Nicholas Burns and Indian Foreign Secretary Shivshankar Menon hold four days of

[143] Chronology of the Indo-U.S Nuclear Deal Available at http://m.times of india.Com/world/US/Chronology-of-the-Indo-US-nuclear deal/articleshow/3575350.cms acessed on 8-5- 2014.

meetings in Washington on the U.S India Civilian Nuclear Cooperation initiative.

- July 27, 2007:- Negotiations on a bilateral agreement between the United States and India conclude. Burns, head U.S negotiator says that the agreement is consistent with the Hyde Act.[144]

- March, 7-14, 2008:- The CPI writes to the Prime Minister Singh, warns of withdrawal of support if government goes ahead with the deal and puts political pressure on Manmohan Singh government not to go with the deal.

- April 23, 2008:- The Indian government says it will seek the sense of the House on the 123 Agreement before it is taken up for ratification by the America Congress.

- June 30, 2008:- The prime minister says his government is prepared to face parliament before operationalizing the deal.

- July 8, 2008:- Left parties in India withdrew support to government.

- July 9, 2008:- The draft India-specific safeguards accord with the IAEA circulated to IAEA'S Board of Governors for approval.

- July 10, 2008:- Prime Minister Manmohan Singh calls for a vote of confidence in Parliament.

- July, 22, 2008:- Government is willing to look at "possible amendments to the Atomic Energy act to ensure that the country's strategic autonomy will never be compromised, says Prime Minister Singh.

- July 22, 2008:- The UPA government led by Manmohan Singh wins trust vote in Lok Sabha in India.

---

[144] Timeline of U.S-India Nuclear Talks available at http://www.USnews.com/news/world/articles/2007/08/28/timeline-of-US-India-nuclear-talks, acessed On 08-05-2014.

- Sep 11, 2008:- President Bush sends the text of the 123 Agreement to the US Congress for final approval.

- Sept. 26, 2008:- PM Singh meets President Bush at the white house, but was not able to sign the nuclear deal as the congress did not approve it.

- Sept. 27, 2008:- House of representatives approves the Indo-Us nuclear deal. 298 members voted for bill while 117 voted against.

- Oct. 1, 2008:- Senate approves the Indo-US civil nuclear deal with 86 votes for and 13 against.

- Oct 4, 2008:- Secretary of state Rice visits Delhi but was not able to sign deal.

- Oct 8, 2008:- President Bush signs legislation to enact the land mark US India civilian nuclear deal.

- Oct. 10, 2008:- The 123 Agreement between the two countries is finally operationalized between them. The deal was inked by the Indian External Affairs Minister Pranab Mukherjee and his counterpart secretary of state Condoleeeza rice in Washington DC.[145]

5.6 SPACE COOPERATION.

The two countries India and USA have had long history of cooperation in civil space arena. India's space-launch vehicle technology was obtained largely from foreign sources, including the United States, and forms the basis of its intermediate range Agni ballistic missile booster, as well as its suspected Surya intercontinental ballistic missile program. India is today see to maintain one of the world's most advanced space programs.[146] Over the last four decades, India has

---

[145] Syed, Muzaffar H. n-3, PP-103,104.

[146] Kronstadt. k.Alam. Indo-U.S Relations, ERS Report for Congress. August 12, 2008. PP- 43, 44.

achieved significant progress in design, development and operation of space system, as well as using the systems for vital services like telecommunications, television broadcasting, meteorology, disaster warning and natural resources survey and management. Towards this it has established operational space systems such as INSAT and IRS and means to launch these space craft through PSLV (Polar Satellite Launch Vehicle) and GSLV (Geosynchronous Satellite Launch Vehicle.)[147]

The Cooperation in space between India and U.S once came to the force under the aegis of the NSSP. The U.S India working group on civil space cooperation (JWG) was established in 2004 and its inaugural meeting was held in Banglore in 2005.[148] During the March 2006 summit, a number of symbolic gestures were also agreed upon to highlight the new era of cooperation between the two countries. These included negotiating of MOUS to place instruments provided by the U.S national aeronautics and space administration, negotiations (NASA) on India's Chandrayaan-1lunar mission, negotiations on space launch agreements and discussions on promoting interoperability between India and US civil space-based positioning, navigation and timing system.[149] The success of Chandrayaan-I lunar mission particularly the joint effort made by the India and U.S scientists helped to find the presence of water on the lunar surface, an important discovery for the world. It is expected that in this arena the cooperation is likely to extend a great deal.[150] In 2007, a meeting of the US-India joint working

---

[147] Syed, Muzaffar H. n-3, P- 69.

[148] Indian Space Research Organization Relaese. "Meeting in India-US Joint Working Group On Space Held At Banglore, July 1, 2005. Available online at http://www./sro.org/press release/Julo1-005.htmml, acessed on 29-04-2014.

[149] US Bureau of Oceans, Environment and Science Fact Sheet, US-India Space Cooperation 2 March 2006, available at http//www.state.gov/P/sca/rls/fs/20 06/62489.html, accessed on 01- 05-2014.

[150] Lele A Jey and Mishra Archana. "Indo-US Strategic partnership: Beyond the

group on civil space cooperation was held in Washington, where officials expressed satisfaction with growing bilateral ties in aerospace field.[151]

5.7 HIGH TECHNOLOGY TRADE AND COOPERATION.

The India -U.S science and Technology cooperation Agreement was signed on October, 2005. This is the umbrella agreement for driving the science and technology agenda under "Indo-U.S strategic dialogue". Subsequently two nations agreed to setup an Indo-US Science and Technology commission.[152] U.S commerce Department officials have sought to dispel "trade-deterring myths" about limits on dual-use trade by nothing that less than 0.5% of total U.S trade value with India is now subject to licensing requirements and that the great majority of dual-use licensing applications for India are approved (about 95% in 2007). Between 2003 and 2007, processing time for dual use applications dropped by 37% to 33 days on average.[153] In 2005, the inaugural session of the U.S-India High Technology Cooperation Defense Working Group was held under High Technology Cooperation Group auspices. Commerce Bureau of industry and security formally designated India as an eligible country under its "validated End-

Nuclear Deal,"Asia Pacific Journal of Social Sciences,"Special Issue No.1, December, (2010):2.

[151] Kronstadt, K.Alam. n-35, P- 44.

[152] India-U.S, Science and Technology, Relationship available at https://www.indiaembassy.org/pageeees.pl….. acessed on 09-05-2014.

[153] U.S Department of Commerce Bureau of Industry and Security, U.S-India High Technology Cooperation group, "The Annual U.S-India High Technology Cooperation Group (HTCG)," Available online at http//www. Bis.doc.gov/international programs/htcw- archives.html.accessed on 09-05-2014.

user" program in October 2007. This designation will allow certain trusted India buyers high technology goods without an individual license.[154]

Since 1998, a number of Indian entities have been subjected to case-by-case licensing requirements and appear on the U.S export control "Entity List" of foreign and users involved in weapons proliferation activities. In 2004, as part of NSSP implementations, the United States modified some export licensing policies and removed the Indian Space Research Organization (ISRO) headquarters from the Entity list. Further adjustments came in 2005, when six more subordinate entities were removed. Indian entities remaining on the Entity list are four subordinates of the ISRO, four subordinates of the Defense Research and Development Organization, the Department of Atomic Energy entities and Bharat Dynamics Limited, a missile production agency."[155]

---

[154] Lele, A Jey and Mishra, Archana. n-27, P- 102.

[155] See Commerce's Entity List at http://www.bis.doc.gov/Entities.acessed on 30-04-2014.

Chapter 6th

CONCLUSION

No two countries are as misunderstood by each other as the United States and India. The misunderstanding goes back to a period after world war Kind, to period when India achieve its independence from colonial rule and the United States as emerged one of the global superpowers. The historical links between the United States and India can be traced to the year 1492, the when Christopher Columbus discovered America in the course of his search for new route to India. Prior to the Indian Independence India had no diplomatic relations with U.S.A, because India's foreign policy was guided and controlled by the British government in those Days. America had also adopted the policy of insulation before the world war (1914-18). She had no interest in any other country of Asia except China and Japan. The two great religious leaders in India Swami Vivekananda and Swami Ram Tirtha visited America and removed many misunderstanding about Hindu religion and Culture in the minds of the America people by their speeches.

In 1911 Lala Hardayal had founded a Gadar party in America and prepared thousands of Indians for the liberation struggle of their country. But they did not succeed. The formal relations of diplomatic relations began after India gained independence. Before this, "American contacts with India had started before the American revolution through soldiers and sea men who had lived both in the American colonies and in India. During the last quarter of the eighteenth Century, several American ships visited Indian ports in connection with trade, could hardly present a true picture of India to America. Shortly after American Revolution, the first American merchantman landed at Indian ports, first at Pondicherry Calcutta. Legal authority to Indo-U.S trade was given by Jay's Treaty of 1794 between England and America. American trade with India a part of the "China trade," continued to be important through the years of the nineteenth century and the clipper ship era. There after it languished and was succeeded by other types of business relationships in late nineteenth century and into the twentieth century.

Later, both countries had mutual contacts through various agencies such as missionaries, tourists, intellectuals and Indian freedom fighters. In 1815, the American Mahratia Mission was established. Missionary activists gave first-hand information about India to the Americans. Their main interest was to establish schools and distribute religious literature. They worked among the poor. They did a lot of humanitarian work during famines of 1897 and 1899. On their return home, the Missionaries condemned India for lack of education, poverty and superstition. The number of missionaries in India rose from 394 in 1892 to 2478 in 1922.

Of India's political leaders, Lala Lajpat Rai was the first to visit the United States. In 1905 he went America in order to tell the American people about the need for Indian Independence. The United stated of America: Hindus impression book written by him was published in America in 1916. He was much influenced by American life and American democratic institutions. He felt that the Indian student could learn a lot from the United States. Lajpat Rai spent five years in America and many attracting many American leaders to sympathize with Indian national position, including T.T Sunderland, a Unitarian Minister who had visited India in 1895-96 and later 1913-14. In 1919 Sunderland wrote India in Bondage, which received an enthusiastic welcome in India.

The best known Indian after Lajpat Rai to promote the cause of Indian freedom was Taraknaath Das. He was the second man to become a U.S citizen (1914), the first being Akshay Kl Majumdar. The United States was a sanctuary for Indian freedom fighters. These included scholars, journalists, scientists and thinkers.

The message of President Wilson delivered in the Congress was a source of great inspiration to the Indian freedom fighters. In-spite of the contribution of the American people towards India's struggle for freedom, the attitude of the U.S Government was discouraging. The U.S Government did not want to displease the British Government. But Mahatma Gandhi emphasis on non-violence and his unique method of fighting British rule through Satyagraha attracted attention of the American people. The Second World War marks the beginning of Indo-U.S. official relations. In 1941, the U.S Government agreed with India and Britain for the exchange of diplomatic personnel. In October 1941, Thomas H. Wilson was appointed the first U.S commissioner in New Delhi: Sir Girja Shanker Bajpai was appointed India's Agent General in Washington. He was to act under the overall supervision of the British Embassy.

Soon after the independence of India, however, relations between India and the U.S took a downward turn. The downward turn continued for nearly half a century. The reasons lie in the narrow view of the world held by then secretary of state, John Foster Dulles and the failed policies of India's first Prime Minister Pundit Jawaharlal Nehru. However, the U.S policy of non-alignment did not match together and became their major source of difference. The refusal of India to join the military alliances sponsored by the United States and different stands taken by it on various international issues like recognition of the Communist China, the Korean Crisis, The American Vietnam war, and the Afghan crisis were quite annoying to American leaders. On the other hand the American support to Pakistan on the Kashmir issue in security council and grant of military aid to Pakistan with a view to meet the Communist threats, support to Pakistan on Bangladesh issue were quite irritating to the Indian leaders. Indo-American relations reached a low point reached a low point during the 1971 Bangladesh war. India supported Bangladesh's struggle for freedom from Pakistani war of genocide. America "tilted" to the side of Pakistan.

Indo-American relations became very cordial during the Kennedy period. His successor, President Johnson also kept the cordiality intact by establishing the Tarpaper Atomic Plant and by supplying a large quantity of food grains to enable India to fight over all the acute shortage caused by the severe drought in 1996-67. Again in 1973, as a friendly ge4sture, the United States wrote off the largest amount of foreign debt ever cancelled ever in history by liquidating two-thirds of its accumulated rupee holding ($2 Billion) in India acquired in return for wheat shipments under PL-480. Again, in 1978 President Carter paid a good will visit to India to register and restore American sympathy and amity for India. Its economic aid, suspended since Bangladesh crisis, was resumed and The U.S government agreed to supply the fuel for the Tarpaper plant. Clearly, carter was predisposed to look India as the leader of South Asia, but unfortunately these brief intervals of warmth were soon followed by bouts of bitterness and disillusionment for one reason or another.

However, since the early eighties, India has been perusing a well-planned policy of improving and strengthening relations with United States. The visit of Indira Gandhi to America in 1982 worked as "operation defrost" between two countries. The improved process continued after Rajiv Gandhi took over in 1985 .His visit to America in June 1985 was a smash hit .The memorandum of understanding regarding technology transfer was a definite landmark .The dramatic improvement in the superpower relationship since 1986 removed the cold on the constraints on the upgrading of Indo-U.S relations. This process acquired a new momentum after the cold war in 1989. Several major changes took place in the world in the beginning of the twentieth century. The Soviet Union disintegrated and the cold war came to its end. The world became unipolar .The U.S became superpower and the leader of this unipolar world .Narsima Rao became the Prime Minister of India in 1991 and in 1992 Bill Clinton was elected as the President of the U.S .All these changes, having a global character, affected one another and marked a new beginning in the Indo – U.S relations .In 1994

Narsimha Rao visited the United States. In March 2000, Bill Clinton came to India and in September 2000, Atal Bihari Viajpayee visited the United States. In Janauary 2001, Geroge w. Bush succeeded Clinton as the next President of the United States, who looked for a good relationship with India. From July 1998 to September 2000, ten rounds of talks were concluded between ten rounds of talks were concluded between Jaswant and Talbot top foreign policy leaders in both countries, to lay the new and intensified grounds of Indo-U.S relations.

The nuclear tests conducted in May, 1998 drew a sharp reaction from the United States, leading to a temporary disruption in the thawing Indo-U.S restrictions and the imposition of a broad range of U.S restriction on India. However the generous offer of help from India to the Unit4ed States following the September 11, 2001 terrorist attacks on the United States as appreciated by Christina B. Rocca, U.S. Assistant Secretary for South Asian Affairs was splendid act of solidarity with American people at the time of urgent need. President Clinton visited India on March 21, 25, 2000, the U.S presidential visit to India after a gap of 22 years. The two countries agreed to cast aside, the doubts of the past and to chart a new purposeful direction in bilateral relations in order to build a closer and qualitatively new relationship between the two largest democracies in the world.

In a meeting between President Bush and Prime Minister Vajpayee in November 2001, the two leaders expressed a strong interest in transforming the U.S-India bilateral relationship. High level meetings and concrete co-operation between the two countries increased during 2002 and 2003. In January 2004,the U.S and India launched the next steps in strategic partnership," which was both a milestone in the transformation of the bilateral relationship and a blueprint relationship for its further progress.

In the process of building this strategic alliance step by step that the political transformation took place in May, 2-4, with the defeat of the BJP. Led government and formation of the UPA, government, Dr. Manmohan Singh became Prime Minister of India. In July, 2005, Bush hosted Prime Minister Manmohan Singh in Washington D.C. The two leaders announced the successful completion of the NSSP, as well as other agreements which further enhanced co-operation in the areas of civil nuclear, civil space and high technology commerce. A statement of intent was signed by Prime Minister Manmohan Singh and President George W. Bush on July 18, 2005 to allow India to have access to civilian nuclear technology. It is important to note that this agreement was signed despite India not been a signatory to the Nuclear proliferation Theory, a global dictate on non-proliferation. The Indo-US deal also makes India's nuclear weapons program acceptable, legitimate and non-threaten to the existing nuclear order unlike those of Iraq, North Korea and Iran. The nuclear deal also seeks to enhance India's nuclear security via nuclear arms control. Condoleezza Rice's visit in March, 2005 and George Bush in 2006 visited India and Indian National Security Advisor M.K Narayan's team visit to U.S.A were instrumental in solving many issues and problems in the Indo-U.S Civilian Nuclear deal. George Bush and his subordinates critically tried to implement the nuclear deal in 2008. The communist parties tried there level best to stop the nuclear deal. Finally they more withdraw this outside support to the congress government and opposition political parties were brought the non-confidence motion on Manmohan Government in Parliament. Less than half of the members opposed the government, but Manmohan win the no confidence motion. Finally Oct. 2008 President Bush signed legislation to enact the landmark US-India Civilian nuclear deal.

Over the past decade, they revised and expanded their understanding of and familiarity with one another. India's Strategic location and geographic proximity to the Indian Ocean, its vibrant and growing economy provides undeniable opportunities for developing special relationship United States. It is important to factor in the fact that no political bilateral relationship is permanent in the long run. Still it could be safe to say that the alignment between India and the U.S is now an enduring part of the international landscape of the 21st century.

Bibliography

- Aiyar, Vidya Shankar. Prime Time Deal. Ed., Chari P.R. Indo-US Nuclear Deal, Seeking Synergy in Bilateralism. New Delhi:Routledge Publishers, 2009.

- Alam, Badrul .Mohammad. Indo-US Relations: Dimensions and Emerging Trends. New Delhi: Shipra Publications, 2013.

- Brown, W.Norman. The United States of India and Pakistan. Cambridge: Mass publication, 1963.

- Chakravarthi, Rekh. Internal Road blocks to the Indo-US Nuclear Deal Ed. Chari.R. Indo-U.S Nuclear Deal: Seeking Synergy in Bilateralism.New Delhi: Routledge Publisher, 2009.

- Chaturshreni, Ved Vati. Indo-US Relations. New Delhi: National Publication1987.

- Chintamani Mahapatra. Indo US-Relations into 21st Century. New Delhi: Knowledge World. 1998

- Dilip, M. India USA and the Emerging World Order. Baroda: University of Baroda, 1995.

- Dixit, J.N. My South Block Years: Memories of Foreign Secretary. New Delhi, Mumbai etc: UBS Publishers, 1996.

- Malhotra,V.K. Indo-US Relations in Nineties. New Delhi: Anmol Publications, 1995.

- Yadav Surya and Narain Yadav India's Nuclear Policy: Compulsions, Commitments and Constraints. New Delhi: Jnanda Prakash, 2009.

- Dutt ,V.P. India's Foreign Policy in a Changing World. New Delhi: Vikas Publication, 1999

- Gandhi ,Prem P. India-US Economic Relations: A Perspective . Ed. Kapur, Ashok. Malik,Y.K. India and USA in Changing World New Delhi : Sage Publication, 2002

- Jaim, Shankar.S. India and USA: new directions,Ed. Sinha, Atish and Mohta Mahup. Indian Foreign Policy: Challenges and Opportunities. New Delhi: Academic Foundation, 2007.

- Kapur, Ashok and Malik ,Y.K. Gould, Harld A and Rubinoff, Arthur G. India and United States in a Changing World. New Delhi: Sage Publication, 2002.

- Karat, Prakash. "Subordinate Ally: Implications of the Indo-US Strategic Alliance," "The Marxist," Vol. XXII, No. 1, January- March, (2001).

- Kaul, T.N. Reminiscence Discree and in Discreat. New Delhi: Lancer Publisher, 1982.

- Khanna V .N. Foreign Policy of India. New Delhi: Vikas Publication

- Limaye, Satu P. US Indian Relations: The Pursuit of Accommodation. Boulder:West View Press, 1993.

- Louscher, David J, Cook, and Alethia H, Military. Relations between the US and India Assessment Prospects, Ed. Kapur.Ashok. Malik, Y.K, India and United States in Changing US-Relations. Ed.Dr. Vinay Kumar. Indo-US Relations in Nineties. New Delhi: Sage Publications, 2002.

- Malhotra ,Vinay Kumar. US Latest Initiatives on Non-Proliferation in South Asia and Indo U.S relations. New Delhi: Anmol Publication, 1995.

- Mohan C. Raja. India and the Emerging Non-Proliferation Order: The Second Nuclear Age Ed. Pant, Harsh V. Indian Foreign Policy in a Unipolar World, New Delhi: Routledge Publishers, 2009.

- Mohan, C. Raja. The Evolution of India's nuclear Doctrine. Sinha, Atish, Mohta, Madhup. Indian Foreign Policy Challenges and Opportunities, New Delhi: Academic Foundation, 2007.

- Natrajan, L. American Christian Mission in India in the 19th Century Modern review Calcutta). July 1964.

- Patil, V.T and Assiananda, Sri. Case Study of US South Asian Relation1942-1965. New Delhi: Minerva Press, 2002.

- Prasad, Bimal. India's Foreign Policy. New Delhi: Vikas Publishing House, 1979.

- Verma, H.M and M.M. Kulshrestha. Approach to Indian Foreign Policy and World Affairs,.Gwalior: Nidhi Prakashan, 1997-1998.

- Purushathaman. D. India's 123 Nuclear Agreement With the U.S. Ed., Pilali, Manmohan. B and Premashekhra. L. Foreign Policy of India Continuity and Change. New Delhi: New Century, 2010.

- Rai,K.Ajai. India's Nuclear Diplomacy After Pokhran II. New Delhi : Darling Kindersley, 2009.

- Rana, A.P. Four Decades of Indo US Relations. New Delhi: Har Anand Publications1994.

- Shukla ,Subhash. Foreign Policy Of India. New Delh: Anamika Publishers , 2007.

- Sinha, Ajoy.Indo U.S Relations, New Delhi: Janki Prakashan, 1994.

- Syed, H Muzaffar. Indo-US Relations. New Delhi: Orange Books International, 2012.

- Tewari, S C. Indo US Relations 1947-1976. New Delhi: Random Publishers, 1977.

- Tewari, S.C. Indo-US- Relations1947-1976. New Delhi: Radiant Publishers, 1977.

- Zia, Rakib Ahmad. International Relations: Theory and Practice. Srinagar: Ali Mohammad and Sons, 2006.

Journals

- Clifford E. Singer. Jyotika, Saksena "Feasible Deals with India and Pakistan after the Nuclear Tests; the Glenn Sanctions and U.S Negotiations," Asian Survey, Vol. 38, No.12, Dec.

- Jha, Nalini Kant. "Reviving US-India Friendship in a Changing International Order" Asian Survey, Vol. 34, No. 12, Dec. (1994).

- Karat Prakash. "Subordinate Ally: Implications of the Indo-US Strategic Alliance," The Marxist, Vol. XXII, No. I, January-March, 2006.

- Lele A Jey and Mishra Archana. "Indo-US Strategic partnership: Beyond the Nuclear Deal, "Asia Pacific Journal of Social Sciences,"Special Issue No.1, December, (2010).

- Malone, David M. and Mukherjee, Rohan . "India U.S Relations: The Shock of the New." International Journal, Vol. 64, No. 4, Autum (2009).

- Malone, David M. and Mukherjee, Rohan. "The Shock of the New" Canadian Journal, Vol. 64 International, No. 4, Autumn (2009), Canadian International Council Ltd.

- Mistry,Dinshaw. " Diplomacy Domestic Politics and US-Indian Nuclear Agreement," "Asian Survey," Vol. 46, No.5, September-October, (2006).

- Ramtanu Maitra. "Clinton and Vajpayee move to Strengthen Indo-American Relations," EIR, Volume27, No. 14, April7,(2000)

- Siva Kumar D. "Sending Indian Troops To Iraq and Indo-U.S Relations," "Third Concept, Vol. 24 No. 285, November (2010).

- Siva Kumar. D, N. "Indo-US Relations in Perspective," Third Concept, Vol. 23, No. 270, August.

- Sivakumar,. "Indo-US Relations during the NDA Regime," Third Concept," Vol. 23, No. 271, Sep.

Online Sources

- Chronology of the Indo-U.S Nuclear Deal Available at http://m.times of IndiaCom/world/US/Chronology-of-the-Indo-US-nuclear-deal/articleshow/3575350.cms accessed on 8-5 2014.s

- Http// en.m.wikipedia.org/wiki:/India-united states-relations. Access on 23-02 2014.

- Http// en.m.wikipedia.Org/wiki/india-united states-relations. Accessed on 17-03-2014.

- http://www.idsa-india.org/an-jun-6.html. Accessed on 22-03-2014.

- Htpp/www.Ph.gov.av/About/Parliamentary-Library/Pubs/rp/rp0102/02rp20/ accessed on 09-04-2014.

- Http/www.gwu.rdu/sigur/assets/docs/scap/scap22-Ollapally. Pdf

- http:/www.dsca.mil/programmes/biz-ops/facyts-book/fiscal year series-2010 Pdf, accessed on28.04.2014

- Http://www.Whitehouse.gov/news/releases/2005/07/2000507186.html /. Accessed on 03-05-2014.

- Indian Space Research Organization Release, "Meeting in India-US Joint Working Group on Space Held At Bangalore, July 1, 2005. Available online at http://www./sro.org/press release/Julo1- 2005.html, accessed on 29-04-2014.

- India-U.S, Science and Technology, Relationship available at https://www.india embassy.org/pageeees.pl…. accessed on 09-05-2014.

- See Commerce's Entity List at http://www.bis.doc.gov/Entities.acessed on 30-04-2014.

- Timeline of U.S-India Nuclear Talks available at http://www.USnews.com/news/world/articles/2007/08/28/timeline-of-US-India-nuclear-talks, accessed on 08-05-2014.

- U.S Department of Commerce Bureau of Industry and Security, U.S-India High Technology Cooperation group, "The Annual U.S-India High Technology Cooperation Group (HTCG),"Available online at http//www.Bis.doc.gov/internationalprograms/htcwarchives.html.accessed on 09-05-2014.

- U.S –Indian Armies wrap up historic exercises by Fred W.Barker III Oct. 2009, Available on http:/www.army.mil/article/29473/UD-Indian-armies-wrap-up.historic-exercise/carnegiee

- URL/www.idsa-India.org/an-de-00-8.html/ accessed on 06-04-2014.

- URL/www.acronym.org.UK/spvisit. Html accessed on 06-04-2014.

- US Bureau of Oceans, Environment and Science Fact Sheet, US-India Space Cooperation 2 March2006, available at http//www.state .gov/P/sca/rls/fs/2006/62489.html, accessed on 01-05-2014.

ABOUT THE AUTHOR

The author is presently pursuing Ph.D. in political science from D.A.V.V University (Davi Ahilya Vishwavidyalaya) Indore-India. He was born in 16th of November 1988 in a small village called Nowpora Tujar Sopore in the northern district of Baramulla of the state of Jammu and Kashmir. He stated from a govt. school and had his B.A and B.Ed. from Kashmir University. He completed his M.A in political science from Barkatullah University Bhopal and M.Phil from D.A.VV Indore. Besides his ongoing studies he is working as an assistant professor of Political Science in the Govt. Law College Indore and also teaches political science at the School of Law D.A.V.V University Indore as a visiting faculty.

www.ingramcontent.com/pod-product-compliance
Lightning Source LLC
Chambersburg PA
CBHW050427290526
45786CB00003B/1424